I

Keep

Asking

Encounter Ministries

is devoted to encouraging people to know and love God. We accomplish this by serving you with . . .

♥ Concerts
♥ Drama Presentations
♥ Short term mission trips
♥ Weekly devotionals (sent over the internet)
♥ Community Outreach
♥ Public speaking (Conferences, retreats, special events)
♥ Materials (books and CDs) to encourage spiritual growth

Dan York—Director of Encounter Ministries

Encounter Ministries is a nondenominational evangelical Christian organization located in Tigard, Oregon. If you would like more information about our ministry please write to: Encounter Ministries/12350 SW Tiedeman Ave./Tigard, OR 97223; email us at: reveration@encounterministries.com; or call us at: (503) 620-4081.

I

Keep

Asking

Daniel York

I Keep Asking
First Printing
Copyright © 2001 by Daniel York

Published by Encounter Ministries with Norseman Ventures Publishers
Printed by Central Plains Book Manufacturing, Winfield Kansas.

ISBN: 1-893186-05-9
Library of Congress Control Number: 2001094025

York, Daniel L., Born October 29, 1958-
    I Keep Asking
        1. Spiritual Growth   2. Christian Life
        3. Worship and lifestyle   4. Devotional

Most *italicized* words represent uncommon words whose definitions are provided in Appendix 1, pages 216, 217.

To Kathleen, my Lady Bluebird, my devoted wife and terrific mother to Bryan, Sarah and Stephen. Amos 3:3

and

To Brian Haller, a champion, best friend, and faithful servant of God, at home in heaven. **"And Jonathan had David reaffirm his oath out of love for him, because he loved him as he loved himself"**—1 Samuel 20:17.

Special thanks to Oswald Chambers whose inspirational writings have challenged me to run after God with increasing passion; to Jeff Davis for his publishing expertise and assistance; to Brian Pautz for editing and formatting as well as writing the prologue; to Kathleen for proofreading; to Chris Breithaupt for designing the book cover; to my classmate, Doug Heckman, for helping bring this dream to reality; and finally to Jesus Christ Who inspires me with His love and gives life its true meaning.

PROLOGUE

Did you know that one of the most effective teaching methods is to ask a person a probing question so as to motivate self discovery?   Jesus understood that a well-worded question could bypass mental resistance and reach the individual's heart effecting lasting change. With the Holy Spirit's promise to teach us, asking questions for the sake of self evaluation and even conviction promises an even greater potential for growth.

Asking why you should read this book, and you should ask that question, is important because you are going to be spending time with the thoughts and recommendations of a man you probably do not know. As the book of Proverbs implies, you become like the people you spend your time with.

It would be my recommendation that in the case of this book and it's author, Dan York, your time will be well spent and the results of this literary relationship will be very fruitful indeed. If you want to grow in the Lord, this book will strengthen your effort and propel you in the right direction. It will increase your commitment to hang in there. If you need comfort, hope and some clues to fitting life's puzzle together, you will find in these pages, markers along the narrow path that leads to life.

Jesus told many stories and used metaphors to come in the back door of our souls and provide a fresh look at His purposes in us. With this in mind and in keeping with the intent of this book, consider with me the Christian life as a metaphor of a ship moored in a harbor. It is owned by a very generous and loving Master Who has assigned you to be its Captain. You are a steward of His property. Your vessel is equipped for battle and is capable of venturing into challenging waters over long periods of time. There is an agenda and rules for travel but amazingly you can choose to stay or venture out.

Unfortunately, ignoring their commission, many choose to stay close with lines tightly affixed to the pier. Provisions are easily acquired, things can be kept clean and tidy and there is rarely any risk from the sea. Minimal labor is needed and much time is afforded to making things look good, keeping entertained and maintaining friendships. The presumed safety is fraught with subtle dangers such as the tendency for comparison, complaining and for complacency.

Eager for you to experience His blessings, the Owner of the ship regularly urges you to launch out. After all, He has equipped you to go to sea. The vessel you are in charge of, though beautiful to look at, gains its true beauty when it sets sail. In a disingenuous manner, many will leave the harbor with great pomp and boasting of ability. Yet once away from the shore, they never set sail for fear of straying too far from the comforts of the familiar. It's nice to be the captain of your ship, but it may seem too daunting a task to venture into the depths of the unknown leaving all behind to follow the Owner's desires. Similarly, people can look as though they are seeking God's direction through the practice of religion but because of disobedience suffer in their relationship with Him. Many actually refuse His influence and control over their lives by failing to commit their sails to the protection of the Holy Spirit.

If you wish to experience the blessings of God, then you must cast off the ropes that bind you to the world and get moving. You must leave the dock and put up the sails so that the wind of the Holy Spirit can direct your life. This book will encourage you to venture out. It will provide direction as you pass through the narrow channel out to sea. I believe you will hear the inspiring cheer to let out your sails so that God may take you where He will for His glory. May your journey be joyful!—Brian Pautz, Editor

CONTENTS

CONTENTS CONTINUED

INTRODUCTION

> The supreme matter in this life and world for all of us is to realize our relationship to God.—D. Martyn Lloyd-Jones in *Studies in the Sermon on the Mount*

On my bedroom wall behind the door are scads of pencil markings left by my three children. These are marks that measure their physical growth. We all enjoy watching these marks progress higher up that white-painted wall. Wouldn't it be something if we could track on a wall our spiritual growth? A friend of mine, Brad Stewart, sent me an e-mail message that in the business world it is a well-known dictum that "you can't improve what you can't measure." If we desire to measure our relationship with God, we need to establish what spiritual growth looks like. But first we need to answer the question, "**Why is spiritual growth important?**"

Fortunately for us, God answers this question in the Bible. Contrary to what many people think, this treasured book is not a collection of antique wisdom sayings irrelevant to our daily living. Just ask those in countries where it is forbidden to own a Bible, how applicable and relevant they find it! The Bible communicates from Genesis to Revelation why we should want to know God. First, He created us to have a loving relationship with Him. Unlike everything else He made, we are specially formed in His image (Genesis 1:27). Spiritual growth is all about love! Love doesn't grow without spiritual effort.

Julian of Norwich wrote in the classic **Showings,** "The love of God is at the center of all things." God absolutely and unequivocally loves us! He created us to enjoy a relationship of intimacy. His plan is that we would be timeless family members. He is all-knowing and all-powerful. He works perfectly and is totally holy. His presence is awe-inspiring and overwhelming. Were it not for Jesus, we could not even come before Him. To neglect loving Him would be like deciding air is not valuable and refusing to breathe!

Second, as we will discover, the Bible communicates that God advocates our spiritual growth. If we want to please and approach Him relationally, we must obey His terms. After all, He is our Creator! We want to grow because it is in His best interest and, therefore, our best interest.

Today, I believe there are several reasons spiritual stagnancy is so commonplace among God's children. For those who live in affluence, there is often little perceived need for a close relationship with God. For those who are self-centered and basically lazy, it takes too much effort to be like Him. Ultimately our real problem, if we are not determined to love and pursue Him, is that we don't truly understand who He is and what He is about! "**The Light shines in the darkness, but the darkness has not understood it**" (John 1:5).*

If you can think of a good reason not to know God, then you don't <u>know</u> God. If you want to know Him better, then you truly are cognizant of life. For what purpose would we really have other than to know and love our Maker—the One Who loves us! Pastor Henry Blackaby said it so well, "A love relationship with God is more important than any other single factor in your life."

This book is the first of a two part volume written as a collection of devotions arranged around the theme of spiritual growth. Specifically in *I Keep Asking,* and in Volume 2, *I Pray Also,* we want to look at three areas: **What Helps Us**

*Unlike the style used by today's translators, I have capitalized all references to God to assist in establishing context and because I personally believe references to Him should be capitalized out of respect and adoration.

Grow; Obstacles to Growth; and, **How We Know We're Growing.**

I assume you already love God and have begun a relationship with Him—whether it is a brand new or quite seasoned friendship. My hope is that you and I will deepen and fortify our relationship with Him. My prayer is that these writings will prime our pumps that we might be filled to overflowing with our sacred Living Water!

The Apostle Paul poured out his life to help others find Christ and follow after Him. Studying his prayers throughout his letters across the New Testament, we find a man who devoted much of his prayer life to asking God to develop the spiritual lives of those to whom he had the valuable privilege of ministering. Paul prayed, in Ephesians 1:17--**I keep asking that the God of our Lord Jesus Christ, the glorious Father, may give you the Spirit of wisdom and revelation, so that you may know Him better.** From this verse comes the title of this book—*I Keep Asking.* One of the best things we can do for each other is pray that God will give us the Spirit of wisdom and revelation so that we will know Him better! Is this not the ultimate purpose of our lives? May He use these reflections to take us deeper in our walk with Him.

Our aims in natural life continually alter as we develop, but development in the Christian life is an increasing manifestation of Jesus Christ.—Oswald Chambers in *So Send I You*

LAYOUT

Before reading on let me explain the layout you will encounter as you read through this book and my reasoning behind organizing the book the way I did.

♦ **Our Focus** boxes: Scripture readings are woven into every topic we will examine. I have carefully tried to ensure that passages used are not lifted out of context. There always lurks the danger that in establishing my agenda I select Scripture verses that support what I want to say. I have deliberately evaluated each topic so that it conforms first and foremost to what God says consistently in His Word. The purpose of the Focus boxes is to sharpen our understanding (vision) by directing us to pertinent thoughts the Bible provides regarding the issues we examine. Never accept any author's writing without cross-checking to ensure that God's Word is not being violated, misused or misrepresented!

♦ **Inspiration/Definition** sections: I frequently collect witty or well-articulated sayings. I have provided this section for each topic simply as a resource for those of you who enjoy compiling quotations and like the mental stimulation that comes from reading what others have to say.

♦ **Consider** sections: At the end of each topic in Part I, I have provided specific action(s) that can be taken to further our growth.

♦ **Markers**: In Part III, I highlight spiritual markers that will better enable us to evaluate our growth process.

As you read through this book remember that I have not attempted to be exhaustive in my coverage of the selected topics. My intent is to provoke thinking, challenge dangerous perceptions, encourage and hopefully inspire you in your quest to know our glorious heavenly Father. It is my prayer that you will be blessed!

What Helps Us Grow

When I was five years old my parents decided they could save money if they just left me outside on the street to fend for myself. They determined would be a tougher, wiser son fending against nature and man No, of course my parents did not do this! How absurd Parenting involves teaching children skills they will need to survive—like eating, selecting the appropriate clothing hygiene etc. Good parents don't abandon their little ones concluding they will do just fine without parental supervision. They provide, interact and lead in proportion to the aging and maturing process of the child. Likewise, our Lord uses His love and resources to advance our spiritual growth. We need to know this so we don't fall into the trap of thinking spiritual growth is all up to us—that our Heavenly Father is not involved.

What God chooses, He cleanses.
What God cleanses, He molds.
What God molds, He fills.
What God fills, He uses.
--J. Sidlow Baxter

PART I:
I KEEP ASKING--FOR YOUR HEART

When God measures a man, He puts the tape measure around the heart, not the head.—*Pulpit Helps* (June 1998)

The Apostle Paul neatly summed up what spiritual development is all about when He wrote to the Galatians:

I have been crucified with Christ and I no longer live, but Christ lives in me. The life I live in the body, I live by faith in the Son of God, who loved me and gave Himself for me (Galatians 2:20).

When I think of focusing on something intently and with passion I am reminded of the greatest basketball player to ever play the game. This man's singular drive propelled him to the top. Along the way he mentored and carried his teammates to multiple championships. You remember this superstar, Michael Jordan. When it came to playing basketball, Michael was all heart.

If a man can be wholehearted in mastering a round bouncing object, imagine giving His heart to know the Almighty. Fortunately, the Bible gives us examples of men and women who did. They were wholehearted in their zeal to know God, people like Joseph, Ruth, Nehemiah, Daniel, John the Baptist, and the Apostles.

Paul was one of the greatest church planters this planet has ever witnessed. When he wrote, "**I have been crucified with Christ and I no longer live but Christ lives in me**," we ought to consider what "**I no longer live**" meant. Paul was opening up his heart and stating emphatically, his agenda, desires, talents, education, family heritage, keen mind and savvy religious connections meant nothing compared to knowing Christ. Paul's ambition was never in doubt—he lived to know Jesus.

A thousand competing voices may clamor for your attention. Most of us do not sit on hillsides tending sheep with time to contemplate the mysteries of God and Who He is. We move at a pace in life that resembles the 400-meter dash. But spiritual growth is not achieved by yelling out "I will get with You later Lord!" as we sprint down our self-made lanes. There are no short cuts to building a strong relationship with Him. We must be willing to focus our minds, our energy and the eyes of our **hearts** on God. We must consistently study what the Word says about Him, spend time in His presence, and be willing to

listen

to what

He

has to

say.

HEART

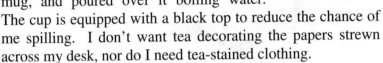

This morning, as per my custom, I placed a tea bag of green tea into a plastic mug, and poured over it boiling water. The cup is equipped with a black top to reduce the chance of me spilling. I don't want tea decorating the papers strewn across my desk, nor do I need tea-stained clothing.

Suppose a small crack developed in my mug. It would be annoying wouldn't it—to contend with a cup that leaked? If holes appeared, I would either have to plug them somehow or throw the mug away.

When I choose to follow Jesus, my intent is that He should have my whole mug—my heart. When He fills me with His Holy Spirit and teaches me through His word, His desire is that I am holy as He is holy. For my heart to function as God intended, I must obey His will!

To give my heart to anything that is contrary to God's will, is like puncturing my mug. The more leaks I spring from selfish desires and ungodly behavior, the less able and willing God is to fill me with Himself. How can I know or serve God if He cannot entrust Himself to me?

Our Focus

Proverbs 4:23—Above all else, guard your heart, for it is the wellspring of life.

God said about the Israelites Moses led out of Egypt:

For forty years I was angry with that generation; I said, 'They are a people whose <u>hearts</u> go astray, and they have not known My ways.' So I declared on oath in My anger, 'They shall never enter my rest'" (Psalm 95:10,11).

Imagine spending forty years with a nation seeking to win their hearts only to find repeatedly that they were more interested in pleasing their own flesh. God was deeply hurt by their self-centeredness. Psalm 78:40 says, **"How often they rebelled against Him in the desert and grieved Him in the wasteland!"**

If we are to find God, we must have hearts that desire Him, hearts devoted to pleasing Him, hearts that beat a steady rhythm of worship!

Is your spiritual mug full of leaks? Are you wanting to be filled to overflowing with the sweet fellowship that comes by spending time with the Lamb of God? Then He must be given the freedom to seal the cracks within your heart.

Inspiration

The heart's testimony is stronger than a thousand witnesses.—Turkish proverb

In other words we have to remind ourselves again that the Christian faith is ultimately not only a matter of doctrine or understanding or of intellect, it is a condition of the heart . . . the heart means the centre of the personality.—D. Martyn Lloyd-Jones in *Studies in the Sermon on the Mount*

The knowledge and vision of God is dependent entirely on a pure heart. —Oswald Chambers in *Biblical Ethics*

Consideration

Having a healthy, crack-free heart for God requires taking inventory of our desires. May I suggest that we consider and write out the desires of our heart. Write out only the desires that pass the following tests with "Yes".

What Helps Us Grow

1. **The Biblical Authority test**. Do I have the mind of Christ in this desire? In other words am I looking at this from a perspective in line with Scripture, consistent with what Jesus would do?

2. **Spousal test.** Do I have the mind of my spouse in this desire? God made us one. Does my spouse agree? {If you are single, have a godly friend or family member evaluate your desire.}

3. **Time test.** Has it been on my heart for a prolonged period of time? In other words this is not a fleeting desire or whim.

4. **The Personal Commitment test.** Am I willing to work at this with all my heart until God either grants my desire or changes my heart? Colossians 3:16.

> Delight yourself in the Lord and He will give you the desires of your heart.—Psa.37:4*

*Abbreviations for Bible books are listed on page 216

19

WILL—SUBMISSION & OBEDIENCE

> If God has not sanctified us and made us blameless, there is only one reason why He has not—we do not want Him to.—Oswald Chambers in *The Love of God Volume: Now Is It Possible*

In truth, our spiritual journey begins when we respond to God's tugging on our heart. Jesus said, in Matthew 6:21— **"For where your treasure is, there your heart will be also."** If God is the One we treasure, then He must have our heart. We would be guilty of self-deception if we claimed we loved Him most but spent our lives chasing other things. Paul wrote in Romans 10:9,10:

> **That if you confess with your mouth, 'Jesus is Lord,' and believe in your <u>heart</u> that God raised him from the dead, you will be saved. For it is with your <u>heart</u> that you believe and are justified, and it is with your mouth that you confess and are saved**.

If we were unwilling to give God our heart, we would not be saved from our sin. Therefore, if we desire to grow spiritually, our will must be engaged so that our heart is able to treasure first and foremost our Father in heaven.

Our Focus

Psalm 40:8—I desire to do Your will, O my God; Your law is within my heart.

John 14:15—If you love Me, you will obey what I command.

Hebrews 12:9—Moreover, we have all had human fathers who disciplined us and we respected them for it. How much more should we submit to the Father of our spirits and live!

I've never put a floating floor in before but in theory it looked simple. All I had to do was line up and glue the tongue and groove wooden slats together tightly and presto my floor should be complete. But by the fifth row of sliding wood together, a problem arose. Gaps were appearing. So I took a hammer and tapped on a metal crowbar against the offending pieces to make them fit. Alas, that resulted in the fragile tongues breaking. The harder I pressed the more damage I caused and the greater my irritation at anything that moved or breathed.

Then I found a wooden block with a groove installed that was meant to help me tap the floor slats into place. If I had taken the time to look for this piece I would not have mangled the wood. Hmm. The best intentions wrongly applied may reap ruin where victory was in sight.

God gives me a beautiful wood block with a groove installed. It is called the Bible. When it is fitted to my life the Holy Spirit is able to tap me into the perfect place of God's will. But when I ignore His will and attempt to do things my own way I end up mangling myself and all that I am next to. Is this oversimplified? Perhaps! But the reality is that without submitting our will to God we can never expect to live in a way that pleases Him. I know what happens when I try to build and don't closely follow the instructions. And I have seen what happens when I negotiate life ignoring the Lord.

To give God my heart implies that He receives it in a condition that He accepts. It would be foolish to think that we can approach our holy God on <u>our</u> unholy terms. So in essence, if I want to know God, I have to approach Him on His terms. We call this obedience. For obedience to be effective, we must first have an attitude of surrendering our will in submission to God's will.

The word "submission" gets a bad rap in our sophisticated age. But there's a "phist" in sophistication that is strongly clenched in pride. It's not brilliance that makes a person resist obeying God, it's pride. I see what my floor looks like when the pieces fit together correctly. To construct a floor properly is a matter of submitting my will to the plans of the architect.

If you refuse to submit to God's will, don't blame Him. Don't fasten the fault on how you were raised. Don't hide behind circumstances or suggest that others are responsible for your misaligned behavior. Take responsibility for that which shapes your every decision—your will! Are you sleeping with someone to whom you are not married? Are you stealing to make ends meet? Are you cheating to get ahead? Are you lying so others think of you more favorably? Do you gossip because it feels good? Do you neglect time with God because you are too busy?

King David knew what sins he was capable of committing. He wisely prayed, **"Teach me to do Your will for You are my God; may Your good Spirit lead me on level ground"** (Psa.143:10). Seek and submit to God's will. Let Him prepare and place you where you should fit. If your will is to do His will, His will is to help you. This might be a good time for confession.

O God, I'm sorry for resisting your will. My desire is to obey You now and forever now. Lead on, O Awesome Father!

Inspiration

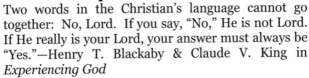

Two words in the Christian's language cannot go together: No, Lord. If you say, "No," He is not Lord. If He really is your Lord, your answer must always be "Yes."—Henry T. Blackaby & Claude V. King in *Experiencing God*

Why did Samuel say that "obedience is better than sacrifice"? Because even in sacrifice there can be the element of self-will. Obedience alone is absolutely honoring to God, for it alone takes God's will as its center.—Watchman Nee in *Spiritual Authority*

Consideration

1. After spending time in quiet meditation does the Lord bring to your mind areas in your life which you need to submit to His lordship? What are these areas? What does He ask of You? Who will you share with in regards to what He is saying to you?

Areas I need to submit to God:

_____

_____

_____

_____

_____

_____

_____

What is God asking me to do?

_____

_____

_____

_____

_____

_____

_____

I Keep Asking

Who will I share with about what God is saying to me?

_____
_____
_____
_____
_____
_____

2.   Make a list of anything that possesses you that you are unwilling to let go of. Ask God what He would have you do.

_____
_____
_____
_____
_____
_____
_____
_____
_____
_____

3.   Ask a close friend if he or she has observed a pattern or attitude in your life that suggests you are unwilling to let go of something.

Holy Father, please help me to submit to You that I would serve in accordance with Your will for Your glory. Help us all, Your children, to wear submission as a blessing that the world might see what it looks like when You do Your perfect work in us!

CONFESSION

Our Focus

Matthew 13:15—For this people's heart has become calloused; they hardly hear with their ears, and they have closed their eyes. Otherwise they might see with their eyes, hear with their ears, understand with their hearts and turn, and I would heal them.

Submission requires relinquishing pride. It's not easy to swallow pride. It's even harder I think to say, "I'm sorry". Do you know any parents who have no contact with their children or vice versa, because one member of the family was offended by the other member but refuses to apologize? What a tragedy it is when a family is destroyed because there is complete unwillingness to admit to any wrongdoing.

My wife does not allow us to put dirty dishes back in the cabinet. If we did we would contaminate the clean dishes. If we want to have a vibrant walk with our Lord, we need to have clean hearts. He will not fellowship with us if we are living in sin. Ezra wrote:

O LORD, God of Israel, You are righteous! We are left this day as a remnant. Here we are before You in our guilt, though because of it not one of us can stand in Your presence" (Ezra 9:15).

King David confessed his adulterous sin before God, proclaiming, "**Create in me a pure heart, O God, and renew a steadfast spirit within me. Do not cast me from your presence or take your Holy Spirit from me**" (Psa.51:10,11).

John wrote, "**If we confess our sins, He is faithful and just and will forgive us our sins and purify us from all unrighteousness**" (1 John 1:9). Confession is mandatory if we want to be near God. It is essential as we proceed along life's journey. "**If**" is a conditional word that implies a need for action. "**Is**" renders a present ongoing truth (faithful and just) of our immutable God. "**Will**" is the promised action guaranteeing forgiveness and purification to all who confess. God established a terrific means for us to have our sins resolved. We merely need to have the humility to confess what is wrong.

There is great release in confession. <u>Don't</u> go another day in sin, confess and believe that God's grace is bigger than your wrongdoing. Then enjoy the refreshment that comes in being able to draw near to God with a pure heart.

Matthew 5:8--Blessed are the pure in heart, for they will see God.

Inspiration

Why not now, in a humbling sense of confessed sin, bow down under the mighty hand of God that where sin abounded, He may make grace much more abound.—Oswald Chambers in *My Utmost For His Highest*

I don't think many of us Christians take confession seriously enough. If we did, our lives would be radically different. When you're totally honest about your sins, something happens. About the fifth day in a row that you have to call yourself a liar, a greedy person, a manipulator or whatever, you say to yourself, "I'm tired of admitting that. With God's power, I've got to root it out of my life."—Bill Hybels in *Too Busy Not to Pray*

Consideration

So when was the last time someone asked you the hard questions:

1. Is there sin you are hiding from God that is eating you alive inside?

2. Are you engaged in activity that you know to be wrong?

3. Is your conscience clear before Your Father who sees all things?

What is the Holy Spirit impressing upon you to confess?

_____

_____

_____

_____

4. Ask someone you know and trust to honestly give feedback if he or she sees an area in your life that is not in accordance with God's will.

Lord, I do love You and I do want to know You. Please forgive me for _____.

Cleanse me and make me new. I repent of my wrongdoing and commit right now in submission to Your will to follow You as best I can in Your strength.

CHARACTER

> Character must be attained, it is never given to us.—
> Oswald Chambers in *The Shadow of an Agony*

My wife chuckles whenever I am scheduled to travel. She laughs because she knows what a procrastinator I am when it comes to packing. I can't tell you how many times I've just made it to the airport because I waited to the last minute to shower and get everything ready.

We can haphazardly grow in our spiritual life more by accident than anything else if we don't take the time to prepare. But that's not a great approach is it? Just as I should prepare before I travel, so I need to make preparation for the journey of walking with God. The author of Hebrews encourages us to:

> **. . draw near to God with a sincere <u>heart</u> in full assurance of faith, having our <u>hearts</u> sprinkled to cleanse us from a guilty conscience and having our bodies washed with pure water"** (Heb.10:22).

It's time to wash, get clean and make preparations for drawing near!

Our Focus

2 Timothy 2:20,21—In a large house there are articles not only of gold and silver, but also of wood and clay; some are for noble purposes and some for ignoble. If a man cleanses himself from the latter, he will be an instrument for noble purposes, made holy, useful to the Master and be prepared to do any good work.

English class plebe year—now there was a challenge! Lots of young men and women enter West Point straight out of high school with outstanding grades. They think they can write. I know. I was one of them. When I heard about how tough it was to pass the first written assignment I didn't believe it could happen to me. I did not carefully follow the instructions my professor handed out because I thought I already knew how to write well. At least until I got my paper back with a big red-lettered "F". And I wasn't alone—95% of the class failed. It was the English Department's standard way of getting our attention. We thought we were prepared because of how well we had done in high school. But they wanted us to write according to a standard with which we were not accustomed.

Let's suppose our character is like a written composition. We set aside God's standards because we think our own effort is sufficient. It's no wonder we get hammered. "I'm a pretty good person" doesn't impress God. Neither does justifying our style. We must strip ourselves from relying upon <u>our</u> thoughts, <u>our</u> standards. Then and only then are we positioned to rely on God's thoughts. Once we see His standards, we can begin to rewrite our character under the tutelage of the Holy Spirit.

Oswald Chambers wrote in *Approved Unto God*, "My spiritual character determines the revelation of God to me." We want God to examine our character. After all, I may be a wonderful person in public and a depraved misfit in private. God sees all. He will not reveal Himself to us because we fool the crowds. He will not make Himself known because of what others think of us. He reveals Himself to us as we conform our character to be like Jesus. Only then can we make His grade!

Inspiration
God does not make us holy in the sense of character; He makes us holy in the sense of innocence, and we have to turn that innocence into holy character by a series of moral choices.—Oswald Chambers in *My Utmost For His Highest*

The foundation, which seems so insignificant and unimportant because it is out of sight, is nevertheless the most vital and important thing of all. If the foundation is wrong, everything else must be wrong.—D. Martyn Lloyd-Jones in *Studies in the Sermon on the Mount*

Consideration

1. What do you think are the weakest areas of your character?

_____
_____
_____
_____
_____

What are your strongest areas?

_____
_____
_____

2. Write down at least three Scriptural themes that are important for understanding and applying in order to get to know God (for example: holiness, love and grace). Number them in the order of which has the highest priority in your life. Then consider how you can improve in each one.

1)._____
2)._____
3)._____

3. How prepared are you to grow? What steps have you taken to allow yourself opportunity and time to get to know your Heavenly Father?

_____
_____
_____
_____

REVERENCE

I want to share with you a Scriptural theme that is hardly ever mentioned today, yet, is critical if we want to grow deep spiritually. Next to love, this is my favorite Biblical theme. If you were to do an extensive amount of research you would find there aren't enough books to fill one shelf on this particular subject. I'm referring to the fear of God. Solomon, the world's wisest man said **the fear of the Lord is the beginning of wisdom**. Since knowing God requires wisdom, the Bible is alerting us to a profound spiritual truth!

Our Focus

Psalm 25:14—The Lord confides in those who fear Him; He makes His covenant known to them.

Jeremiah 5:22—"Should you not fear Me?" declares the Lord. "Should you not tremble in My presence?"

Jeremiah 32:39,40—I will give them singleness of <u>heart</u> and action, so that they will always fear Me for their own good and the good of their children after them. I will make an everlasting covenant with them: I will never stop doing good to them, and I will inspire them to fear Me, so that they will never turn away from Me.

Reveration* means reverent-adoration. It is a word I created after studying for years the fear of God. If love for God is food then reverence for Him is water. We need both to nourish our relationship. Love devoid of respect is emotionally immature causing people to perceive God as some sort of cosmic genie. Respect without love is mechanically rigid such that people approach God from a sense of duty, concerned about failing, convinced that He is a harsh Judge.

**Single italicized words* are defined at the end of the book in Appendix 1.

31

While living in the Sinai desert for six months, I read through my Bible and highlighted in red pencil every reference to revering the Lord. Over 286 verses in 44 of the 66 books of the Bible address fearing Him. The application of reverence has powerful implications for us.

Acacia tree in Sinai desert

The key to salvation is found in the fear of God—**"He will be the sure foundation for your times, a rich store of salvation and wisdom and knowledge; the fear of the Lord is the key to this treasure."** (Isaiah 33:6). The Apostle Paul wrote in 2 Corinthians 7:1, **"Since we have these promises, dear friends, let us purify ourselves from everything that contaminates body and spirit, perfecting holiness out of reverence for God."** This makes sense doesn't it! God is awesome. Who would approach the President of the United States wearing shoddy clothes! Why then should we think we can "hang" with the Lord in a cavalier, slipshod manner? If we devalue Him, we reveal our ignorance towards His awesomeness. Our motivation to be holy and pure is due to our deep respect for God's all-surpassing greatness. We confess our sins and work on developing strong character not just so we can be clean but because we recognize the value of being like our Savior.

The more I experience God the more He overwhelms me! How humbling it is to consider that this perfect, all-knowing Lord would value me so highly as to let His own Son be murdered for me. I'm staggered by the faithfulness of a Father I don't deserve. I'm thrilled by the touch of an invisible Holy Spirit Who warms me like no fire can.

The secret to knowing God requires fearing Him. Will He grow close to those who disrespect Him? How do we feel when we are taken for granted? Will He embrace men and women who use His name in vain? God yearns for our heartfelt piety. When we come before Him with awe and treat Him with the majesty He deserves, He blesses us in ways we could never have imagined. Mighty King David prayed, **"Teach me Your way, O Lord, and I will walk in Your truth; give me an undivided <u>heart</u>, that I may fear Your name"** (Psa.86:11).

*Give me an undivided **heart** O Lord! Don't let the cravings of my flesh turn my core into a leaking vessel of shame! Create in me a wholehearted love for You that gives off the aroma of a joyful attitude and blesses Your palate with the rich taste of godliness that comes from obedient service and a humble spirit. Fill my cup Lord, for Your glory.*

Inspiration

The remarkable thing about fearing God is that when you fear God you fear nothing else, whereas if you do not fear God you fear everything else.—Oswald Chambers in *The Pilgrim's Song Book*

If the majority of us worked for our employer the way we work for God, we'd be fired before the week was out.—John Bevere in *The Fear of the Lord*

Let deep fear of the Lord and dread of all that might displease or grieve Him fill you. Then shall you never have any evil to fear . . . The childlike believing fear of God will lead you into the love and joy of God.—Andrew Murray in *The New Life*

Consideration

Let me encourage you to take your Bible and read it in its entirety for the next year. Each time you come across the fear of God highlight it in colored pencil or underline it. I believe you will come away impressed and challenged to revere the Lord. The following year you might want to pick a different theme and follow the same plan!

ABIDING

> I think God is crying out and shouting to us, "Don't just do something. Stand there! Enter into a love relationship with Me. Get to know Me. Adjust your life to Me. Let Me love you and reveal Myself to you as I work through you." A time will come when the doing will be called for, but we cannot skip the relationship. The relationship with God must come first.—Henry T. Blackaby & Claude V. King in *Experiencing God*

♦ A bag-lady leans forward on a rotating stool in the corner of the brightly-lit casino feverishly slapping quarters in the machine she desperately hopes will be her savior. Her sallow cheeks betray the expense of her abiding.

♦ A middle-aged man stares into the glare of his 17-inch monitor. He searches endlessly for more pornographic pictures--aroused on a hunt he hopes will never be discovered. His face burns as warm as the guilt that flows through his heart at the cost of his abiding.

♦ A father wearily enters his home at an hour long after his children have gone to bed—a pattern triggered by his love for work.

♦ A family forsakes Sunday worship all summer because a forest, a coast and a river camping site are more fun.

♦ A teen finds his Bible boring compared to *Dungeons and Dragons.*

♦ A Christian businessman knows the stats on every player the Yankees fielded the last ten years but he is clueless how to find Deuteronomy.

In God's family photo album what are we doing in most of the pictures? One thing is certain if we want to draw close to Him, we better not waste our time where He has no interest in being.

Our Focus

John 15:5,9—I am the vine; you are the branches. If a man remains in Me and I in him, he will bear much fruit; apart from Me you can do nothing . . . As the Father has loved Me, so have I loved you. Now remain in My love.

Abiding is another theme that resonates throughout Scripture with respect to knowing God. To remain in Christ is to abide with Him! Jesus says we cannot bear fruit on our own. We cannot please God by our own making. Each year I cut off "shooter" branches on my fruit trees. They may climb high to the sky and look good, but they don't bear apples or plums or cherries. Jesus compared those who refused to remain in Him with worthless withered branches. They are picked up, thrown in the fire and burned. I don't want to be a worthless branch. I imagine you don't either!

When we devote our **will** and our **heart** to Jesus we experience fulfillment in life no fantasy can touch. But if we follow the course of our self-indulging appetites we will end up waving our sorry branches to the theme song—E-M-P-T-I-N-E-S-S. God did not make man from dust to glorify dirt. He made us to bear fruit because we are His friends!

Today you and I have the opportunity to walk and talk with our Father. We can read His thoughts in the Bible. If we listen to what He has to say, He might profoundly speak to us. To the degree that we involve Him in our activities and time we will experience the thrill of His presence. Abide and glide or turn and burn. Sometimes the choices really are simple.

Inspiration

Ask yourself, is this work, this activity, deflecting me from abiding in Christ? If so, then fling it overboard.—Oswald Chambers in *God's Workmanship*

It is well that we accept the hard truth now: *the man who would know God must give time to Him.* He must count no time wasted which is spent in the cultivation of His acquaintance.—A.W. Tozer in *The Divine Conquest*

Consideration—Keeping a Journal

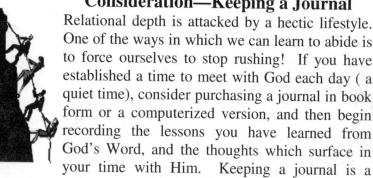

Relational depth is attacked by a hectic lifestyle. One of the ways in which we can learn to abide is to force ourselves to stop rushing! If you have established a time to meet with God each day (a quiet time), consider purchasing a journal in book form or a computerized version, and then begin recording the lessons you have learned from God's Word, and the thoughts which surface in your time with Him. Keeping a journal is a marvelous way to interact with God and to see what He is doing in your life. While I confess it is hard for me to journal, when I do, my times with the Lord are richer. I enjoy typing out prayers to the Lord. This keeps my mind from wandering and enables me to focus more on listening to Him. Try it! I think you'll be encouraged by the results.

DEDICATION

Christianity is not devotion to a cause or to a set of principles, but devotion to a person, and the great watchword of a Christian is not a passion for souls, but a passion for Christ.—Oswald Chambers in *The Place of Help*

Ron York with a Pike

Ron sits in the open craft oblivious to all but the task ahead of him. He stares at the opaque surface so intensely one would swear he sees what others cannot. His hands thread the squirming brandling across the warm metallic hook like some splendid surgeon. With the expert toss of a quarterback, he casts his line precisely to the spot he hopes and waits . . . and waits. If the worm won't deliver, he daps or skitters with a fly he has meticulously crafted. He is unfazed by failure. His arsenal of tricks runs deep from years of careful learning. If patience is a virtue, Ron is the waiting virtuoso. Neither mosquitoes, rain, nor hunger will keep him from his task. He is a fisherman. If you want to catch fish, do as he does.

Anne is the queen of shopping. She finds bargains and buys with unmatched expertise. She buys the Sunday paper on Saturday and utilizes every valuable coupon she can find.

Tim's mind never rests. He knows the talents of his players. His strategic grasp of the game and tactical counters to the moves of opposing coaches has made him a legend among those who love soccer.

Michelle rarely loses a case. She loves defending the helpless victim. The way she fashions words seems magical. Just ask the law students of Clairemont College.

Our Focus

Deuteronomy 6:5-7—Love the Lord your God with all your <u>heart</u> and with all your soul and with all your strength. These commandments that I give you today are to be upon your <u>hearts</u>. Impress them on your children. Talk about them when you sit at home and when you walk along the road, when you lie down and when you get up.

Romans 12:1—Therefore, I urge you, brothers, in view of God's mercy, to offer your bodies as living sacrifices, holy and pleasing to God—this is your spiritual act of worship.

Dedication is not some hidden exit we bypass on the highway of life. We all know what it means to be dedicated. Whether we are wise in that which we avidly pursue is another matter. Paul was so faithful in his dedication to Jesus Christ that he boldly exhorted the Christians in Philippi to live as he lived. The citizen believers in that prosperous Roman colony in Macedonia had a high affinity for the apostle who bore Roman citizenship yet zealously lived for a higher Kingdom. His modeled devotion to God enabled him to say, **"Christ will be exalted in my body, whether by life or by death"** (Php.1:20b).

To be a great fisherman I must make the necessary sacrifices to learn how to fish. If I want to know the Lord Who loves me, I must be willing to study and apply His Word. I must talk and listen to Him. I must learn from those who already know Him well. There are no shortcuts with dedication. Selfless devotion to God begins when we consecrate our lives to Him. It continues as a joyful daily commitment to serve Him in thought and action. It has no ending just like our eternal Father.

What Helps Us Grow

A *quintessential* aspect of dedication involves setting our priorities. God makes us a priority. We know this because of the reality of Christ's dedicated love for us. A good way to understand this is to think of how a parent views his or her children.

Many parents with three or more children learn about the "middle child syndrome" at some point in their parenting journey. Often the oldest child receives attention because he or she is the first to experience new things growing up. The youngest child also gains much attention by virtue of need. Parents can only focus so much attention. Therefore, it is not hard to understand how the middle child can feel left out or excluded, if especially if he or she is fairly self-sufficient.

Sarah holding her cousin Annie

My daughter, Sarah, is our middle child—fast becoming a young lady. It is important to me that I communicate love and devote attention to her—especially because she is sandwiched between two brothers. I make it a priority to enter her world. What kind of parent would I be if I did not make the time to love each of my children to the best of my ability. Likewise, God does not want any of His children to feel left out. When we recognize this fact it should motivate us to spend more time with Him. I see this with Sarah, who shows her appreciation for our relationship by sending me wonderful cards she finds on the internet.

I highly recommend for your reading, *A Father's Reward* "*Raising Your Children to Walk in the Truth*". This is an outstanding book that reveals unvarnished lessons from a dad dedicated to challenging fathers to disciple their own children as God intended. It is written by Phil Downer, the former president of **Christian Business Men's Committee (CBMC)**.

Children left to themselves rarely grow up to be sterling adults. Immoral peers, ungodly teachers, an internal sin nature, and Satan and his vile underlings, are all capable of inciting moral meltdowns.

If you are a parent, before you trot off on another spectacular assignment, or give your best time and energy to work, consider the welfare of your children. God says we are to impress upon them His commandments. What holds and impresses your young ones—the television, computer games, drugs, sex, music, skateboarding, sports etc.? We cannot afford neglecting time with the most precious gifts God entrusted to us. My guess is that if we shirk spending quality hours with our offspring we are shirking quality time with our Father.

Dedication is not mouthing clever creeds or wearing certain clothes or acting as if we are doing God a favor by spending time with Him! Dedication is recognizing we belong to Him and that we had better get serious about prioritizing our life so that God is included in all we do. **It's all a matter of priorities . . . isn't it?!**

Inspiration

Devotion is not a thing that passes, that comes and goes . . . it is something habitual, fixed, permanent that extends over every instant of life and regulates all our conduct.—Douglas V. Steere

. . . the great concern of our lives is not God, but how we are going to fit ourselves to live. Jesus Christ says, "Reverse the order, get rightly related to Me first, see that you maintain that as the great care of your life, and never put the concentration of your care on the other things.— Oswald Chambers in *Studies in the Sermon on the Mount*

Consideration

How can I stay dedicated to God today? Yesterday is history, tomorrow is not here. I only have today!

Imagine yourself in prison, locked up in solitary confinement. You have no Bible. Is it possible to be dedicated to God in such a circumstance? Certainly! God promised He would never leave or forsake us (Psa.94:14). So what can you do?

1. Pray. There are no walls between you and God. **For the eyes of the Lord are on the righteous and His ears are attentive to their prayer . . .** " (1 Peter 3:12)

2. Obey. In thought, word and deed, even confined, you can obey and serve God. (Joshua 24:15)

3. Maintain. Keep your body clean, rested, and exercised. (1 Corinthians 6:19)

4. Witness. You can let your light shine even before your prison guard. (Mat.5:16).

5. Meditate. You can dwell on Scripture your mind recalls. (Jos.1:8)

6. Worship. You can sing for joy to God and glory in Him. (Psa.81:1)

If these are things that can be accomplished locked up in a cell, what is keeping us from being dedicated to our God as His free children?

HOLINESS

> Any Christian who is not earnestly pursuing holiness in every aspect of his life is flying in the face of God's purpose in saving him.—Jerry Bridges

As a child I had a hard time telling the truth. I would often resort to lying because I thought I could avoid being punished. I remember on one occasion when my dad came home and found out that I was fibbing. Now as a parent I understand how my deceit was detected, then as an eight-year old, I was clueless how my parents knew I was guilty!

Dad gave me the standard don't lie lecture. Faced with the reality I'd been caught, I admitted my error. At that point I expected to get spanked. Dad took his belt off and I grimly awaited the punishment I'd earned. But then as if he'd had a change of mind he removed his shirt and set aside the belt. He picked up a paddle once used for bouncing a rubber ball on a string. Then he explained how much it hurt him that I would lie. He said that this time he was going to take my punishment for me. He then handed me the paddle, bent over the bed and told me to hit him. I couldn't do it. He implored me again--firmly, leaving no doubt that I was to administer the blows to his back.

After two feeble pats to his back I was crying harder than I had ever wept for any spanking I'd ever received. I learned a profound lesson that permanently changed my outlook toward lying.

God looked down from heaven discouraged with a world bent on doing evil. He sent His Son to earth so that we might see what holiness looked like. Jesus chose every time to do what pleased His Father. Yet, every day He saw sin all around Him. Though He was perfect and powerful, He did not spank humankind. Instead He allowed Himself to be killed in the most shameful manner by those dead in sin, to rescue us from our most shameful condition. Why? God loves us. He loves us! He loves usssssssss!

If my reason not to sin is to be good or to avoid punishment, I will sin. My selfish nature is too strong. Holiness does not come by simply hating sin. Holiness comes by loving God. Why would I want to do what is wrong and hurt the One Who took my blows to save me?

Our Focus

Hebrews 3:12,13—See to it, brothers, that none of you has a sinful, unbelieving <u>heart</u> that turns away from the living God. But encourage one another daily, as long as it is called Today, so that none of you may be hardened by sin's deceitfulness.

1 Peter 1:15—But just as He who called you is holy, so be holy in all you do; for it is written: "Be holy, because I am holy."

What keeps us from being holy? We can boil the gist of the problem to selfishness but that may be overly harsh. Perhaps what we lack is courage. The Apostle Paul wrote:

I eagerly expect and hope that I will in no way be ashamed, but will have sufficient courage so that now as always Christ will be exalted in my body, whether by life or by death" (Php. 1:20).

Are you willing to let your body be exalted? Live for Jesus! Set aside whatever would cause you to disobey and be holy as He is holy. Let us not be afraid to kill those passions that quench our thirst for our Almighty Friend; that keep us from holy living for Christ--dying for gain.

Inspiration

We have learned to live with unholiness and have come to look upon it as the natural and expected thing.—A.W. Tozer

I have to recognize that sin is a fact, not a defect; it is red-handed mutiny against God, and acquaintance with the grief of it means that unless I withstand it to the death, it will withstand me to the death. If sin rules in me, the life of God will be killed in me; if God rules in me, sin will be killed in me.—Oswald Chambers in *The Place of Help*

Why should we ask that we may be kept from evil? For the great and wonderful reason that our fellowship with God may never be broken. If a man merely wants to be holy as such, there is something wrong with him. Our supreme desire should be to have a right relationship with God, to know Him, to have uninterrupted fellowship and communion with Him.—D. Martyn Lloyd-Jones in *Studies in the Sermon on the Mount*

Consideration

J. Oswald Sanders in **A Spiritual Clinic** asks us to answer the following positive questions so as to determine whether we should engage in a certain activity or action:

1. Will it bring glory to God?
2. Is it profitable?
3. Will it help me in my Christian life, my witness, my service?
4. Does it edify?
5. Does it tend to enslave?
6. Will it strengthen me against temptation?
7. Is it characteristic of the world or of the Father?

Gen. 35:2—**So Jacob said to his household and to all who were with him, "Get rid of the foreign gods you have with you, and purify yourselves and change your clothes. Then come, let us go up to Bethel, where I will build an altar to God, Who**

answered me in the day of my distress and Who has been with me wherever I have gone."

Jacob challenged his family to get rid of their idols, and clean up their act. Write down three things that you do that are not holy.

1._____
2._____
3._____

Share this with your most trusted friend and ask for God's help in eliminating each item. At the end of the week evaluate your progress. If possible, commit your friend to asking you each week how you are doing in your efforts to be holy.

HUMILITY & "POVILITY"

The "3 Amigos"—Dan, Brian and Dave at West Point, N.Y.

Brian Haller died December 12, 1985 one of 248 peacekeepers on their way home after six months of military duty in the Sinai. Brian and Dave Mead were my two best friends. We spent four years together at West Point and almost four years serving in the 101st Airborne (Air Assault) Division. Kathleen and I named our oldest son Bryan David for these inspiring men.

Brian was one of the most humble men I ever had the privilege of knowing. I have met few individuals as discerning and sensitive as he was. He continuously put the needs of others before himself. He wasn't always like that. Dave and I used to give him a hard time over the way he would treat plebes. But Brian grew in humility as he grasped his own condition before the eyes of a holy Lord.

Many a night in the Sinai he settled into his chair exhausted after a hard day of serving his soldiers only to ask how I was doing. If I replied "I'm fine", he knew whether I was holding something back. During a time period when I was wrestling with a major decision that was unpopular in many people's minds, he stood by me and encouraged me. We spent many great hours in the Word and praying for each other's soldiers. What a sensitive heart Brian possessed!

Our Focus

Matthew 5:3—Blessed are the poor in spirit, for theirs is the kingdom of heaven.

CPT Brian Haller—2nd from Left; 4 Company Commanders in the Sinai

Well-intentioned people have taken the first beatitude "Blessed are the poor in spirit" and determined that God's will was that they be poor. Monks in monasteries have sworn vows of poverty forsaking all but minimal essentials by which to live. The belief is that possessions interfere with becoming Christ-like. Ironically, one can achieve poverty just as one can achieve wealth. But was Jesus really calling people to be materially deprived?

Moses taught the Israelites, "**However, there should be no poor among you, for in the land the Lord your God is giving you to possess as your inheritance, He will richly bless you**" (Deu.15:4). The Bible says God "**sends poverty and wealth; He humbles and He exalts**" (1 Samuel 2:7). Indeed He "**secures justice for the poor and upholds the cause of the needy**" (Psa.140:12). But poverty in the Bible was primarily the result of not obeying God's laws and suffering the consequences. In the New Testament neither wealth or poverty was the goal but rather contentment with what one had. So what does Jesus mean by poor in spirit?

Wealthy King David wrote, " **Yet I am poor and needy; may the Lord think of me**" (Psa. 40:17a). Poor in spirit indicates a person's abject humility before an Almighty God. It is a healthy sense of inadequacy and need for the Lord. It is a condition of the heart God applauds.

Jesus says the kingdom of heaven belongs to the poor in spirit. If we want to come before Him, we need to be humble. What a fantastic call for *povility*—the blessed state of humbly recognizing my inadequacy before my Lord; His awesomeness--my neediness.

Inspiration

When it comes to gaining humility, the point is not to win but to lose.—Joni Eareckson Tada in "At the Foot Of the Cross", *Discipleship Journal* Issue 105

Humble people don't think less of themselves . . . they just think about themselves less.—Norman Vincent Peale

There is no-one in the kingdom of God who is not poor in spirit . . . It means a complete absence of pride, a complete absence of self-assurance and of self-reliance. It means a consciousness that we are nothing in the presence of God. It is nothing, then, that we can produce; it is nothing that we can do in ourselves. It is just this tremendous awareness of our utter nothingness as we come face to face with God.—D. Martyn Lloyd-Jones in *Studies in the Sermon on the Mount*

Consideration

An achievement-oriented culture insists that position, accomplishments, power and beauty are what matter most. Unless God has graciously broken us we don't consider being poor in spirit as valuable. "God helps those who help themselves" is a clever saying but it is not found in Scripture. In order to become poor in spirit, we must be broken of every pride that props up "me" at the expense of "Him". Are you willing to pray this prayer?

O God, please break me. Please tear away and uproot anything in my life that keeps You from being Lord. Please do that surgery that only You can do that would allow me to grow closer to You. Father, I don't want to go through tragedy or trauma for You to get my attention. But I don't want to miss you because of pride either. So Father, knowing my heart and what I need, I yield my life to You to do with as You will for Your glory! Amen.

TRUST

Our Focus

Psalm 10:17—You hear, O Lord, the desire of the afflicted; You encourage them, and You listen to their cry.

Psalm 57:4—I am in the midst of lions; I lie among ravenous beasts—men whose teeth are spears and arrows, whose tongues are sharp swords.

He was treated like an outlaw, a condemned man with an entire army pursuing him. Despite the fact that he had committed no crime, the ruler of the land was determined to kill him. With a band of ragtag followers, this hunted young man skillfully moved about always remaining one step ahead of his pursuers tracking his every move.

Consider what obstacles he faced. He had to survive in the En Gedi desert, a place with venomous snakes, scorpions and dangerous animals, where a broiling sun, high desert winds and cold nights made just living a challenge. His emotions plummeted to depression and leaped to joy only to fall again as new obstacles replaced old triumphs. On top of his own needs, he carried the burden of leading and caring for his loyal friends and fellow warriors. Finding food and water was a major challenge. At night they slept the fitful sleep of prey. Every noise could be the advance of an approaching enemy.

One day he found a cave to hide in. His enemies camped outside not knowing he was trapped. Most astonishingly, the jealous king who sought his death came into the same cave to rest. Now the hunter became the target of opportunity. With one quick thrust of a sword the young outlaw could put an end to the mad king obsessed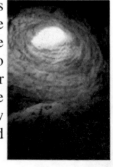

with killing him.

Instead, David spared Saul's life. Rather than act in his human strength to be rid of his master he chose to trust in God Most High, the One:

Who fulfills His purpose for me. He sends from heaven and saves me, rebuking those who hotly pursue me; God sends His love and His faithfulness . . . Be exalted, O God, above the heavens; let Your glory be over all the earth" (Psa.57:2,3,5).

You can read David's cave adventure in 1 Samuel 24.

Certainly David had problems. He also had a steadfast heart capable of generating praise songs in dire occasions. Why? Because beneath the coat of unfair he was forced to wear was a heart that beat the indestructible theme--I trust God! Do you? Do you sometimes feel like a rusted VW Bug trying to avoid being run over by three lanes of SUVs and 18-wheelers? Does life seem unfair? Excellent—now is the perfect time to trust God. You can demonstrate your trust by praising Him! That's right! <u>Praise</u> <u>is</u> <u>a</u> <u>precursor</u> <u>to</u> <u>drawing</u> <u>closer</u> <u>to</u> <u>Him</u>! The best way to engage trust that God is bigger than our problem is to praise Hymn! God, Who fulfilled His purpose in David's life, will fulfill His purpose in your life. Will you let Him? Will you let go of solving problems your way and trust in His way? I hope so—you won't regret it.

Inspiration

It will ever be the first wish of my heart to aid your pious endeavors to inculcate a due sense of the dependence we ought to place in that all wise and powerful Being on whom alone our success depends.—*George Washington to his favorite chaplain, Reverend Israel Evans while alone, cold and discouraged at Valley Forge*

Faith is nothing other than the certainty that God speaks truth . . . No one apprehends anything unless he has the power to

51

believe; he must simply begin and continue saying to the Lord that he is sure that His Word is truth. He must hold fast the promise and rest upon God for the fulfillment.—Andrew Murray in *The New Life*

Consideration

1. What is an area of your life where you need to trust more in God?

_____

_____

_____

_____

What steps are you willing to take that will help you to grow in the area of trust?

_____

_____

_____

_____

Do you use a day timer or planner? Be creative and make an appointment with God to interact with Him regarding this issue. Protect your time with Him. If the phone rings don't answer it. You are meeting with the King of kings!

2. One area where many people have a difficult time trusting God is in the area of finances. Many churches have annual faith-pledges where their members are challenged to give beyond what they think they are able trusting that God will provide. Many ministries depend upon finances that people have in faith pledged to give. Are you willing to be stretched beyond your comfort zone? Spend time in prayer and ask the Lord to lead you in increasing your giving to your church, to missionaries or to a cause He has laid on your heart. Then when you have determined an amount that will test your ability to trust God, begin faithfully setting aside your gift at the beginning of each month before you pay your bills! Give to God first and watch how He blesses your life!

PRAYER

Our Focus

Colossians 4:2—Devote yourselves to prayer, being watchful and thankful.

On top of the hill in a place I have long since forgotten Paul Drake got down on his knees with me and wept in prayer for the city of San Diego and the sailors on the Naval bases where God had led us to minister. I felt like we were a threesome. Why, because the saint next to me conversed so passionately with God to reach the lost for Himself that the Lord had to be right by us. As I think back in my life, the times I have always most clearly sensed God's presence involved praying.

Prayer is nothing to be afraid of; not something to dismiss as some spiritual exercise reserved for professional believers. Prayer is open to us all because our God wants to hear what we have to say and for us to listen to Him. He is not looking for how polished our words are. He is not grading our syntax. He enjoys hearing what is on our hearts.

The man or woman who is devoted to God as evidenced by an effective prayer life, apprehends the mind of Christ. To know the mind of Christ is to discern God's will. It is the practice of prayer that teaches us about the character of God. It is the exercise of prayer that builds up our flabby spiritual muscles. It is the conduct of prayer that ushers us into the presence of the One Who loves to fellowship with us. Without prayer, we are in danger of presumption. We may be guilty of modeling to others that it is our own hard work that accomplishes ministry.

I remember a preacher in seminary who drilled into us the importance of putting long hours into sermon preparation. His teaching was sound but it was devoid of any passion for God. His goal was to move the audience by the beauty of his sermons. Evidently his passion for sermonic excellence was not based on prayerful devotion to God. He left his wife for another woman. Today, to my best knowledge, he has nothing to do with God or ministry.

O God, teach us how to pray! Deepen our longing to come into Your holy presence!

Are you discouraged? Do you claim spiritual "burn-out"? Have you lost your way? Does your walk with God seem flat? Friend, get on your knees right now! Resolve to establish daily time to meet with Your Father in heaven. Be devoted to prayer. Don't talk about it—do it! If you need help find a praying person and become a prayer partner. Be cautious about praying to see God work—that is a weaker reason for going to Him. Pray to know Him. Pray to discover His character and will for your life. If you and I will be faithful to pray, God will revitalize us. He will take us to a deeper understanding of Himself. Then He can use us for the work of His ministry. Then we can say 'Glory!' and know what it means!

Inspiration

 Prayer is the way the life of God is nourished. It is impossible to conduct your life as a disciple without definite times of secret prayer . . . Prayer does not fit us for the greater works; prayer is the greater work.—Oswald Chambers in *My Utmost For His Highest*

Prayer does not change God, but it changes him who prays.—S. A. Kierkegaard

To pray well is the better half of study.—Martin Luther

Consideration

How to Build a Strong Prayer Life

1.   Set aside 15 uninterrupted minutes every day to pray.   If that seems like forever, start with 5 minutes.   The important thing is establishing a habit of talking to God.   As a plebe during Boot Camp, I didn't have 15 minutes available to pray so I got my quiet times in the privacy of the latrine.   There's always a way to get with God we just have to have the desire.

2.   Mary Geegh wrote a terrific little book entitled *God Guides*.   It is the best resource I can recommend for learning how to listen to God.   You can order this book by contacting Marcy Zastrow, PO Box 546, Wausau, WI 54402-0546.   Telephone: 715 845-4011.

3.   Use the Lord's Prayer as a format to help you pray:
Recognize and praise God for His attributes
   Our Father in heaven, hallowed is Your name.

Pray for His kingdom to come.
   Your kingdom come.

Ask for His will to be done in your life
   Your will be done on earth as it is in heaven.

Share with the Lord your needs
   Give us today our daily bread.

Confess any sin the Holy Spirit brings to mind.
   Forgive us our debts as we also have forgiven our debtors

Ask Him to protect you from falling into sin
   And lead us not into temptation

Pray for Him to rescue you from Satan's attacks.

   But deliver us from the evil one. (Mat.6:9-13)

I Keep Asking

Another helpful tool to equip us for prayer is The Navigator's **Hand Illustration** seen below. You can download this illustration by going to: http://www.gospelcom.net/navs/navinfo/resources/prayhand.htm.

4. Keep a prayer notebook of things for which to pray. You might have a section on family, people in ministry, people at work, your neighborhood, teammates, political leaders, personal issues etc. Be creative! You will soon find (if you haven't already), to adequately talk to God about all the issues and areas you've identified will take longer than 15 minutes! So grow that time with Him!

CONVICTION

Setting up signs might seem like an inconvenience to some people, but I relish the job. Every Sunday morning between 7:30 and 8:00 a.m., if I'm in town, I'm loading up our minivan with signs to place strategically near Fowler Middle School. These are special signs. They are invite-people-to-God-hey-community-we-are-gathering-to-worship slabs of wood bonded with plastic proclaiming **Light of Christ Community Church** with direction arrows and time of service.

Now why would I, as a pastor, be out putting up signs? Surely this is a responsibility that should be delegated. Well, maybe so. But until God raises up someone with a heart that rejoices in setting up signs, He's given me a strong sense of conviction that I'm to do it! I'm setting them up for Him. There is no such thing as an unimportant task if it is done for the Lord.

Bill Cosby once said, "There's no labor a man can do that's undignified, if he does it right." If for some reason I don't set out the signs, I've had people in our community ask me, "Is your church still meeting? Is everything okay?" I can tell you lots of folks have come and worshiped with us because they saw our sign and responded. The simple act of advertising resulted in someone joining us for fellowship to worship God!

Our Focus

Ezekiel 4:9—Take wheat and barley, beans and lentils, millet and spelt; put them in a storage jar and use them to make bread for yourself. You are to eat it during the 390 days you lie on your side.

God asked His prophet Ezekiel to do some pretty bizarre things. Read Ezekiel chapters 4 and 5. Amazingly, Ezekiel complied with the Lord's strange requests. If you and I will respond to the convictions He lays on our hearts we will see Him do amazing things in our lives. If God gives you a conviction, it is for your betterment. So don't argue with Him. Don't rationalize why someone else should do what He's asked you to do. Don't complain about how you've had to work so hard and nobody appreciates your effort or that the work is beneath your stature! Don't make excuses with your all-knowing Creator. Don't wimp out! Be faithful.

Whether God calls us to some task or to change our attitude, if His Holy Spirit has impressed upon our heart the rightness of an action we must do it. This is what assists us in growing closer to Him. If He sees that we are faithful and obey the conviction He gives us, He is able to reveal even more of Himself to us. The sooner we figure this out the quicker we can get on with walking with Him. Are there signs He wants you to put up? Then get on with it—for His glory!

Inspiration

Never discard a conviction. If it is important enough for the Spirit of God to have brought it to your mind, it is that thing He is detecting.—Oswald Chambers in *My Utmost For His Highest*

A belief is something you hold; a conviction is something that holds you.—Jerry Bridges

Consideration

Identify and write out seven major convictions you hold. For example, Job said, "I made a covenant with my eyes not to look lustfully at a girl" (Job 31:1). _____
_____
_____
_____

What Helps Us Grow

_____

_____

_____

_____

_____

_____

Next ask the Holy Spirit to reveal any area in your life around which you need to establish a conviction. Are you watching R-rated movies that contain sex and excessive violence? What does the Lord have to say about this? Are you guilty of stretching the truth to suit your needs? Are you willing to have your neighbor over to build a relationship and share the gospel but television is interfering?

_____

_____

_____

_____

_____

_____

Share what the Lord has impressed on your heart with your spouse or someone you know who might benefit from what God is teaching you.

DISCERNMENT

> ## Our Focus
> Proverbs 16:21—The wise in heart are called discerning, and pleasant words promote instruction.

The art of discerning is comprised of two parts—keen insight combined with good judgment. Spiritual discernment occurs as the Holy Spirit gives insight to a person regarding a particular situation or individual(s). Therefore, as a person grows closer to God, the ability to discern should also blossom. We need discernment to sense what God is telling us. We need discernment to keep our heart centered on the Lamb of God.

The closer we walk with Jesus the better we are able to identify what is good versus what is harmful, what is best versus what is adequate—both in ourselves and for others. Discernment enables us to be like the chess player who sees five moves in advance. In essence, as we rely on the Holy Spirit to lead us in the daily pursuit of serving God, He gives us insight into the five big W's (who, what, where, when, why). Does this mean we always know what to do or what lies ahead—certainly not! Even in the fogbanks of life, we are not lost for discernment also consists of faith. *Impalpable* circumstances should lead us to our knees in pursuit of God's faultless leading!

Discernment must always be exercised with humility. Just because we are privy to insight does not give us the right to speak—this is where judgment kicks in. Proverbs tells us even a fool is considered discerning if he knows when to keep silent (Pro.17:28). In exercising wisdom or *sagacity* we must also be sensitive to avoid becoming critical. There is no profit to be gained in finding fault in others but there is great honor in going before God's throne on another's behalf.

What Helps Us Grow

One aspect of discernment that we often overlook is the art of asking questions. Notice some of the questions Biblical characters felt free to bring before God.

Psa.10:1—**Why, O Lord, do you stand far off? Why do You hide Yourself in times of trouble?**

Jer.12:1—**You are always righteous, O LORD, when I bring a case before You. Yet I would speak with You about Your justice: Why does the way of the wicked prosper? Why do all the faithless live at ease?**

Habakkuk 1:13—**Your eyes are too pure to look on evil; You cannot tolerate wrong. Why then do You tolerate the treacherous? Why are You silent while the wicked swallow up those more righteous than themselves?**

Mat.13:10—**The disciples came to Him and asked, "Why do You speak to the people in parables?"**

Mat.17:19—**Then the disciples came to Jesus in private and asked, "Why couldn't we drive it out?"**

Have you ever felt restricted from asking God questions that burn inside your heart? Is there a sense that Christians are supposed to have all the answers—that questioning is a sign of immaturity? I, for one, am skeptical of those who always seem to know exactly what to do. Sometimes even a "spiritual" bucket can contain hogwash.

Of course not every question is appropriate. Solomon noted, **"Do not say, 'Why were the old days better than these?' For it is not wise to ask such questions"** (Ecclesiastes 7:10). Sometimes instead of seeking to know what God wants, we veer into the realm of complaining. Bottom line: If we want to know God's thoughts on life, we need to feel free to ask Him our honest questions! He is bigger than all our *humongous* dilemmas.

Life is full of quandaries. Better to be honest about what we don't know than to give the appearance that we have all the answers. Better to go to God then to pretend we don't care.

Inspiration

The situation today is Lots of knowledge, but little understanding
Lots of means, but little meaning
Lots of know-how, but little know-why
Lots of sight, but little insight.—Robert Short

Discernment of God's truth and development in spiritual character go together.—Oswald Chambers in *Approved Unto God*

All ecstasies and experiences, all inner voices and revelations and dreams must be tested by the pure outer light of Jesus Christ and His Word.—Oswald Chambers in Christian Discipline

Consideration

Henry Blackaby in his book, *Experiencing God* shares seven realities that are excellent in helping us experience God. Let's use these seven realities to help us become more discerning.

#1. "God is always at work around you." What work is God doing around you right now?

_____

_____

_____

_____

(When I first moved to Tigard, Oregon, it became very evident to me that people loved to play soccer. I felt the Lord's leading to start a soccer league in order to form relationships among people my age. It was a natural and effective ministry because it served an obvious felt-need. From that ministry I have made friendships that have led to my being able to share the gospel message.)

#2. "God pursues a continuing love relationship with you that is real and personal." What can you look back upon in your life and see as evidence that this is true?

_____

_____

_____

_____

#3. "God invites you to become involved with Him in His work." What do you sense God would have you do right now in your life?

_____

_____

_____

_____

#4. "God speaks by the Holy Spirit through the Bible, prayer, circumstances, and the church to reveal Himself, His purposes, and His ways." (We will study this in Part I of *I Pray Also*). What has the Holy Spirit said to me recently through:

God's Word?_____

_____

Prayer?

_____

_____

Circumstances?

_____

_____

Other believers?

_____

_____

#5. "God's invitation for you to work with Him always leads you to a crisis of belief that requires faith and action." What crisis of belief are you facing right now? _____

_____

_____

What do you need to trust God for?

_____

_____

What action do you sense God wants you to take?

_____
_____
_____

#6. "You must make major adjustments in your life to join God in what He is doing." What major adjustments do you need to make? _____

_____
_____
_____

#7. "You come to know God by experience as you obey Him and He accomplishes His work through you." Are you experiencing God? Are you living in obedience to His Word?

_____
_____

Let's pray Paul's prayer:

And this is my prayer: that your love may abound more and more in knowledge and depth of insight, so that you may be able to discern what is best and may be pure and blameless until the day of Christ (Php.1:9,10).

DUTY

Often when people ask me how I am doing, I will respond by saying, *"Better than I deserve."* It is not a response I created. I learned it from Paul Drake. When asked how he is doing, whether circumstances are good or trying, Paul can be counted on to say, *"Better than I deserve."*

Our Focus

Luke 17:10—So you also, when you have done everything you were told to do, should say, "We are unworthy servants; we have only done our duty."

John 12:26—Whoever serves Me, must follow Me; and where I am, My servant also will be. My Father will honor the one who serves Me.

Duty is a tough word and a resilient concept. *The American Heritage Dictionary* defines it as 1. "An act or a course of action that is required of one by position, social custom, law, or religion: *Do your duty to your country.* 2.a. Moral obligation".

Robert Boardman served with the Marines during World War II. Bob lost a finger and had his throat shot through by the single round of a sniper on the island of Okinawa. After the war, rather than bemoaning his lost voice and becoming bitter towards the Japanese he chose to give his heart to Christ for foreign missions. Many people were stunned when Christ led him to serve as a missionary in Japan.

The Lord used a gravely voice from a giant man to communicate what His love is all about. You can bet that when he speaks, those in close proximity listen! Bob, you see, is the personification of duty. He would not let his feelings get in the way of obeying what he knew God wanted him to do.

I Keep Asking

As an officer with the Army reserves I am constantly in contact with young soldiers. Today it is sad how few young people coming in to the military have learned the true meaning of duty. You see, when the economy is cranking and people are well off, duty is set aside for convenience. Personal satisfaction, the "right to play", takes priority over the compulsion to meet a moral/job-related obligation. If you want to measure the state of a society, sample its sense of duty. The spiritual health of a church can also be gauged according to its faithfulness to obey God or its penchant to do only what is appealing.

Those who model a strong sense of duty have good hearts and a healthy understanding of grace. When we appreciate the fact that God loved us so profoundly that He would send Jesus to die for our sins, we have a heightened appreciation for what it means to serve Him! As sinners we don't deserve grace. Yet if our faith is in Jesus Christ, we are justified. We are declared free of blame because He took our sins on His own back. Therefore, when we serve we ought to serve with joy. We ought to work hard and faithfully because no matter what we are going through, we are blessed!

So don't be discouraged! Strive to serve faithfully! By God's grace, you are doing better than you deserve. If you are slacking, get off the bench and back in the game! He who will not serve is not a follower of God but a follower of self. We glorify and come to know God by being faithful and that's something to think about . . . in reveration!

Inspiration

If duty is disagreeable, it is a sign that we are in a disjointed relationship to God . . . Once we become rightly related to God, duty will never be a disagreeable thing of which we have to say with a sigh, "Oh, well, I must do my duty." Duty is the daughter of God. Never take your estimate of duty after a sleepless night, or after a dose of indigestion;

66

take your sense of duty from the Spirit of God and the words of Jesus.—Oswald Chambers in *The Moral Foundations of Life*

If God did not bless, not one hair, not a solitary wisp of straw, would grow; but there would be an end of everything. At the same time God wants me to take this stand: I would have nothing whatever if I did not plow and sow. God does not want to have success come without work, and yet I am not to achieve it by my work. He does not want me to sit at home, to loaf, to commit matters to God, and to wait till a fried chicken flies into my mouth. That would be tempting God.—Martin Luther

Consideration

My friend, Dan Breckel, is a driving examiner. He has some pretty hilarious stories to tell of rookies behind the steering wheel. Dan's duty is clearly defined. He must determine if the one driving does so in accordance with the law and safe driving practices. If not, that person cannot pass the driving test. If Dan did not perform his duty, incompetent drivers would procure driver's licenses and unleash their recklessness upon already congested highways.

In the same way, if we serve competently as Christians with a clear understanding of what God would have us do, we may directly assist a person in coming to a correct understanding of the saving knowledge of Jesus Christ. A bad witness for Christ is a poor representation of God and His standards.

Let me encourage you to take and apply a prayer that means so much to me. It is an old prayer infused with an eternal message of rightly doing one's duty. Dan and I were taught this prayer as cadets at West Point.

The Cadet Prayer

O God, our Father, Thou Searcher of Human hearts, help us to draw near to Thee in sincerity and truth. May our religion be filled with gladness and may our worship of Thee be natural.

Strengthen and increase our admiration for honest dealing and clean thinking, and suffer not our hatred of hypocrisy and pretence ever to diminish. Encourage us in our endeavor to live above the common level of life. Make us to choose the harder right instead of the easier wrong, and never to be content with a half-truth when the whole can be won.

Endow us with courage that is born of loyalty to all that is noble and worthy, that scorns to compromise with vice and injustice and knows no fear when truth and right are in jeopardy.

Guard us against flippancy and irreverence in the sacred things of life. Grant us new ties of friendship and new opportunities of service. Kindle our hearts in fellowship with those of a cheerful countenance, and soften our hearts with sympathy for those who sorrow and suffer.

Help us to maintain the honor of the Corps untarnished and unsullied and to show forth in our lives the ideals of West Point in doing our duty to Thee and to our Country.

All of which we ask in the name of the Great Friend and Master of all. Amen.

PART II: OBVIOUS OBSTACLES TO GROWTH

> Growth for the sake of growth is the ideology of the cancer cell.—Edward Abbey
>
> Our toils to rectify sin are themselves twisted by sin, our labors to shed light on iniquity themselves darkened by iniquity.—J. Budziszewski in *The Revenge of Conscience*

One of the reasons why I quote Oswald Chambers so frequently is that he seemed to have an uncanny eye towards those things that keep us from growing in Christ. But he never let obstacles become a reason to stop growing, stop teaching others, or stop worshiping God. He wisely wrote in *My Utmost For His Highest:*

> The river of the Spirit of God overcomes all obstacles. Never get your eyes on the obstacle or on the difficulty . . . Never allow anything to come between yourself and Jesus Christ, no emotion, or experience; nothing must keep you from the one great sovereign Source.

Have you ever walked on ice? The Japanese have developed a nifty invention for dealing with slippery surfaces. They designed a small rubber sole that can be attached to the bottom of boots. On the rubber sole are two rows of steel teeth which bite the snow and ice when one walks. When I traveled without this device it was very difficult not to slip and slide. Once the grippers were stretched over my boot walking on frozen ground was easier.

Life can be filled with ice-covered pathways. Often we encounter circumstances that require care in negotiating. If we try to overcome them in our own power, we may be in for a fall. If we would take the time to study the Bible, we would discover that it becomes like those grippers. The Holy Spirit gives us wisdom to negotiate treacherous terrain--to negotiate whatever could cause us to slide through the application of His word. But unless we are equipped to walk we are doomed to slip and fall.

Sometimes we cannot avoid obstacles because of the environment in which we live. Other times we need to leave the environment we are in for spiritual growth to occur. At times our enemy attacks us. Still other times we, by our own sin, invite problems. In part two of this book we want to examine obvious impediments to our spiritual development. Let's look together at some of these growth-quenchers.

I'M CONCERNED ABOUT YOUR . . . PRIDE

> The smallest package I ever saw was a man wrapped up wholly in himself.—Reverend Billy Graham

There are moments in life we never forget—life-changing encounters. One of mine came as a "firstie", a senior at West Point. I asked the leader of **Officer Christian Fellowship** (OCF), a personal friend my father had led to the Lord in Okinawa, if he would meet with me to discuss the topic of serving. On the day we met, he looked me in the eye and said, "Danny, we don't need to talk about serving, we need to talk about pride." He then lovingly shared three specific examples of pride he observed in my life from one dinner conversation in his home.

Each example he cited was accurate. His surgery was clean and compassionate. Colonel John George knew malignant pride when he saw it and it was growing in me like rust on metal. I was shaken to the core. I understood from years of reading Scripture that God does not tolerate the proud. The Bible is replete with stories of men and women who were intentionally humbled and in some cases destroyed by God for their rebellious pride. I had no desire to join that list.

Our Focus
Proverbs 29:23—A man's pride brings him low, but a man of lowly spirit gains honor.

There is a good form of pride, that in which a person has dignity and self-respect. Healthy pride takes pleasure in achievement, a possession, or an association—like parental pride. Conversely, there is a dangerous form of pride which when fully grown, displays arrogance, an unteachable spirit, defensiveness, disdainful conduct or treatment of others, and haughtiness.

The prophet Isaiah wrote:

How you are fallen from heaven, O Lucifer, son of the morning! How you are cut down to the ground, you who weakened the nations! For you have said in your heart: 'I will ascend into heaven, I will exalt my throne above the stars of God; . . . I will ascend above the heights of the clouds, I will be like the Most High.' Yet you shall be brought down to Sheol, To the lowest depths of the Pit (Isa.14:12-15—NKJV).

Before God created Adam and Eve, the sin of pride was fully hatched in the heart of Lucifer. He wanted to be like God. He sought to usurp the irreplaceable One. Satan deceived Eve and Adam to ignore the command of God not to eat the forbidden fruit in the garden with the lie that by eating, they too, would be like God. This ought to help us understand why pride is called the root of all evil.

King Solomon wrote, **"When pride comes, then comes disgrace, but with humility comes wisdom"** (Pro.11:2). I owe a debt of gratitude to a man who had the courage to address my character. May I ask you the condition of your life? Are you full of pride? How would those around you answer the question?

Inspiration

Christ sends none away empty but those who are full of themselves.—Donald Gray Barnhouse in *Revelation*

The greatest curse in spiritual life is conceit.—Oswald Chambers in *My Utmost For His Highest*

Why does God hate pride? Because it blocks His children's connection with Him, the only solution to their deepest needs. And pride brings immense loss to God, for it deprives Him of the genuine intimacy with us that He longs for. — Warren and Ruth Myers in "The Joy in Humility", *Discipleship Journal* Issue 105

CRITICAL SPIRIT/JUDGING

Notice:
This office requires no physical fitness program.
Everyone gets enough exercise jumping to conclusions,
flying off the handle, running down the boss, knifing
friends in the back, dodging responsibility and pushing
their luck.—Author Unknown

The surest test to determine if I struggle with pride is to
gauge the acidity of my thoughts toward other people. I
confess I have a long way to go and were it not for Jesus I
would never make it.

I remember the night when three people were insensitive
to the needs of a group I was leading. Rather than address
the offenders firmly with love, I found my thoughts ripping
the leader of the three for her immaturity and spoiled manner.
I lost sleep that night consumed by what they had done
unable to pray for them and to let God reveal the condition of
my own heart.

It is easier to be critical than to be patient. It is easier to
cut apart than to edify those who annoy. It is easier to judge
than forgive. It is easier to water the critical vine with its
"superior" vicious thorns than to yank out the roots of this
bitter-tasting plant. If I harvest its fruit, I will damage my
communion with God, my commitment to others and my
own contentment. The Holy Spirit can eliminate this weed if
I will obey God's Word which says:

**Finally, brothers, whatever is true, whatever is
noble, whatever is right, whatever is pure,
whatever is lovely, whatever is admirable--if
anything is excellent or praiseworthy--think
about such things.—Php.4:8**

It is sad how many Christians who once started zealously
down the path of seeking God now sit on the bench

consumed with bitterness towards others, towards God. Don't become a casualty because it was easier to house unpleasant thoughts than to eliminate them. Did you know that harboring a critical spirit will prematurely age you?

The world is full of "fault experts". If you find yourself adept at spotting weaknesses in others remember the words of Jesus Who said:

And why worry about a speck in your friend's eye when you have a log in your own? How can you think of saying, "Let me help you get rid of that speck in your eye," when you can't see past the log in your own eye? Hypocrite! First get rid of the log from your own eye; then perhaps you will see well enough to deal with he speck in your friend's eye. (Mat.7:3-5 NLT).

Let go of harboring a collection of other's perceived misdeeds. God is able to lead us past the actions or attitudes others exhibit that were reckoned as harmful.

I don't enjoy being in the company of critical people. I find in every work place and home environment where criticism abounds, a heavy cloud of despair and vindictive spirits. When I personally judge others my disposition is unpleasant. The state of being "ticked-off" is never uplifting. Nor am I pleased inwardly with the negative thoughts that circulate.

Fundamentally, the problem with judging is that I take what is God's domain of authority and complete understanding and suppose it is my own. It is an arrogant action on my part for I do not have all the facts and I cannot see inside a person's heart as God does.

Does this mean we are not to speak or weigh-in against the sins of others? No, certainly the Bible is full of examples of godly people renouncing sin. The Old Testament contains numerous accounts of prophets speaking against idolatry and other sins the Jews committed. But Jesus would not let the teachers of the law and the Pharisees rip into a woman caught in adultery (John 8:1-11). He stopped them because their motivation was wrong. They sought to trap Him at her expense. They were not concerned about God's kingdom; they were enamored with their own power. When we pronounce sentence from a motive that is laced with self-interest and far from concern over what grieves God, we have no right to judge. We ought to ask ourselves before we condemn, "Why does this person's sin or perceived wrongdoing <u>really</u> bother me?"

Kindness is a good remedy to a judgmental attitude. Kind actions have an uncanny erasing effect over saber-waving thoughts. But the best remedy to a critical spirit is prayer. The Holy Spirit, our true Heart Physician, sees our deepest motives and reveals our own failings. Only when I am honest before Jesus can I truly pray with discernment over those I previously judged.

Our Focus

Philippians 2:3—Do nothing out of selfish ambition or vain conceit, but in humility consider others better than yourselves.

Inspiration

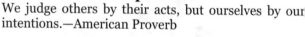

We judge others by their acts, but ourselves by our intentions.—American Proverb

I never met a man I could despair of after having discerned all that lies in me apart from the grace of God. Stop having a measuring rod for others. Jesus says regarding judging, "Don't; be uncritical in your temper, because in the spiritual domain you can accomplish nothing by criticism." One of the severest lessons to learn is to leave the cases we do not understand to God.—Oswald Chambers in *Studies in the Sermon on the Mount*

Everyone in a crowd has the power to throw dirt: nine out of ten have the inclination.—William Hazlitt

Obstacles to Growth

Criticism makes you hard and vindictive and cruel, and leaves you with the flattering unction that you are a superior person. It is impossible to develop the characteristics of a saint and maintain a critical attitude.—Oswald Chambers in *Studies in the Sermon on the Mount*

Hardening of the attitudes is the most deadly disease on the face of the earth.—Zig Ziglar

ADDICTION

Message posted on an internet site for Addiction.

First time here. I got up this morning and decided to seek help. I don't know what made today any different but I'm tired of being the person I am. I am addicted to everything. Alcohol, nicotine, porn, coffee even potato chips. It doesn't matter what it is I over indulge. I think the real problem is that I don't enjoy life and so I'm always trying to escape but I'm 43 years old and I don't enjoy the things I do to escape anymore.

I want my life back. The life I had before my teenage years introduced me to sex, drugs and rock and roll. I can faintly remember a very sensitive, creative, loving, compassionate young boy inside of me that had wonderful, healthy, decent and God-loving dreams about life. Sometimes when I look in the mirror I catch a passing glimpse of that little boy and wonder whatever happened to him. I guess I feel like if I don't do something soon then that little boy will die and I will never have hope.

I think it's time that he and I help each other find life again. Sorry if this post sounds like just mindless ramblings. Maybe it is. I don't know anymore. — Matthew

The Bible emphatically informs us that we who love God are temples of His Holy Spirit (1 Co.3:16). Abusing the temple is a quick way to cut off spiritual fellowship. It's amazing how many ways we can abuse our jars of clay. Consider that:

#1. We need to regularly work out to stay physically fit. When we don't exercise our endorphin and serotonin levels fluctuate such that we are set up for depression or a heightened state of anxiety.

#2. We need to drink enough good water each day. The body needs one pint every 4-6 hours to cool our brain and help the body function correctly. Did you know that it takes an 8-ounce glass of water to flush one cup of coffee through our liver and kidney? We are not hydrating our bodies properly by ingesting coffee and other caffeine-laced beverages.

#3 We need to eat correctly to help our serotonin levels. If our diet does not include fruits, vegetables and plenty of carbohydrates we again are set up for physical problems. There is a reason why God commanded the Jews not to eat pork. Aside from the fact that it is dangerous to eat pork that is not fully cooked, it is the hardest of the meats for the stomach to digest.

#4. We need to get enough sunlight. Sensory Acute Deprivation (SAD) contributes to moodiness and other disorders. My brother will readily attest to the difficulty he experiences battling depression during wintertime in Anchorage, Alaska. Other residents of that beautiful state express the same challenge of living during a season when the sun is gone 20+ hours a day.

#5. We need to get the right amount of sleep—for most people six to eight hours. Too much sleep produces excessive melatonin which makes waking up a real challenge. Not enough sleep reduces the melatonin we need so that it becomes even harder to conk out.*

*Christian Mental Health Counselor Gerry Blankenheim is the source of the information for #'s 1-5.

Our Focus

Proverbs 20:1—Wine is a mocker and beer a brawler; whoever is led astray by them is not wise.

Isaiah 5:11—Woe to those who rise early in the morning to run after their drinks, who stay up late at night till they are inflamed with wine.

Romans 13:13,14—Let us behave decently, as in the day-time, not in orgies and drunkenness, not in sexual immorality and debauchery, not in dissension and jealousy. Rather, clothe yourselves with the Lord Jesus Christ, and do not think about how to gratify the desires of the flesh.

It is interesting that Paul was not writing to unbelievers but rather to fellow Christians when he wrote the exhortation in Rom. 13:13,14. The Roman society he knew had perfected feeding pleasure. No doubt he watched many Christ-lovers fall prey to the temptation to gratify sanctioned lusts. Their addictions then remain our struggles today. But instead of admitting we are chained to evil behavior, we've become quite good at using blame to rationalize addiction. "He was abused as a child—so he can't help being trapped in pornography." While in fact there are chemical traits that pass from one generation to another rendering some extremely vulnerable to alcohol, it still comes down to a choice to pick up that first glass and drink. Virtually all addictions do not happen by accident but rather by choice.

Great Christian homes have been ruined by a dad or mom who started playing the lottery, fell in love with gambling and couldn't stop. How many Christian marriages are wrecked by a spouse secretly smoking joints before graduating to hard drugs? There are men who once hungrily read Scripture who now cannot get enough sports. They can spend hours talking about athletes, purchase season tickets, and yet, have no time for Jesus. Others cannot wait until the office is clear so they can surf from one pornographic website to another. Still others cannot satiate the need to make more money, to buy new and better toys, homes, cars etc. Their journey is perilous for lust is the friend of darkness.

The signs of addiction are plentiful. A person's physiological or psychological need becomes so great that it creates a wall of defense. Those who are addicted often don't think they have a problem—they have rationalized so effectively to the point they believe their own press. They will fight to give up anything. They become secretive, often financially strapped, totally lacking in self-control. Soon anger becomes a common emotion with mood swings that baffle and hurt those who are friends or loved ones.

Christian counselor Gerry Blankenheim said, "A person who has an addiction does not have spiritual growth because that addiction becomes god." In truth addiction is both idolatry and adultery. We bow before that which pleases us and set aside the One we worship for another lover.

It is not hard to become addicted. Have you noticed (how couldn't you!), that drugs flourish in our land? It is fairly easy to obtain Ritalin or Paxil for hyperactive children. It's easy to let the television, computer games or videos assume the role of babysitter. In a fast-paced society that belches stress, drugs like Zoloft become our magic pill that will make bad feelings go away. But how we define and treat our flesh determines the control Lord Addiction will possess. Few talk about the side effects of medication. The siren song of every industry catered to pleasing the flesh minimizes as much as possible describing the long-term consequences of over-indulgence. If you want to avoid becoming addicted you must agree with Paul:

You may say, 'I am allowed to do anything.' But I reply, 'Not everything is good for you.' And even though 'I am allowed to do anything,' I must not become a slave to anything . . . Or don't you

know that your body is the temple of the Holy Spirit Who lives in you and was given to you by God? You do not belong to yourself, for God bought you with a high price. So you must honor God with your body" (1 Co. 6:12,19,20—NLT).

If you are already addicted, seek help. God will be your strength if you will let Him!

Inspiration

The core of any addiction is the same for everyone. It is that void inside of us where we have allowed the world to dictate to us that it has the substance that would fill us.—Dr. Jorge Valdĕs

HOW DOES AN ADDICTION DEVELOP?
It is possible to describe phases in a negative addiction:

1) Experimentation: Urges arise out of curiosity

2) Expected enjoyment: Urges arise out of fond memories of past enjoyment

3) Doing it to cope: Urges arise primarily in response to stress

4) Doing it to survive: Urges are frequent (hourly, doing it as a way of life daily); or urges may be prevented more than they are experienced. Specific stressors are no longer needed as triggers for urges, because the addiction is woven into many or most aspects of life. The addiction helps the addict maintain a sense of stability and normality.—Arthur T. Horvath, Ph.D.

ANGER

USA TODAY, Newspaper Article 4-14-88

Have you ever noticed that sometimes we get angry and remain bitter with people and actually forget why we're so upset? Take, for example, the notorious Hatfield-McCoy feud. It hit newspaper front pages in the 1880's, when the Hatfield clan feuded with the McCoy clan from across the border in Kentucky. Historians disagree on the cause of the feud--which captured the imagination of the nation during a 10-year run. Some cite Civil War tensions: McCoys sympathized with the Union, Hatfields with the Confederacy. Others say it began when the McCoys blamed the Hatfields for stealing hogs. As many as 100 men, women and children died.

In May 1976, Jim McCoy and Willis Hatfield--the last two survivors of the original families--shook hands at a public ceremony dedicating a monument to six of the victims. McCoy died Feb. 11, 1984, at age 99. He bore no grudges--and had his burial handled by the Hatfield Funeral Home in Toler, KY.—Peter Johnson

---

Again and again she tried to shake the hostile thoughts from her head without success. But she could not. The reminder of pain gnawed away at her. The accusing voices stoked embers that would not die. She had not spoken to her children in over five years. In truth she had no idea where they were. She worked hard to convince herself she didn't care. They had hurt her badly and they must pay.

Until one night she saw him in a dream. She found herself alone in what seemed a garden of beautiful roses. Through the only entrance he walked to her confidently. From a distance he looked strong and powerful. His clear voice complimented her for her resolve. He shook his head and spoke disapprovingly of what they had done to her. She blushed and warmed to his approaching steps. Now he was right in front of her. She looked down but his hands pulled her chin up until she could see into his steeled eyes. Then it happened. His face slowly, torturously began to change from what she thought had been a kind smile to an evil sneer. His grip on her face tightened. She could not pull away. As her eyes raced wildly seeking escape she noticed the flowers were bleeding and thorns raced upward until she was completely, hopelessly encircled by their razor barbs. "You call upon me for strength," he roared. "Well I am almost complete and you cannot let me go. You belong to me now."

"Who are you," she meekly cried. He laughed hard at her brier prison. "I am Anger. Behold the thorns that you have grown."

Our Focus

1 Samuel 20:30-33—Saul's anger flared up at Jonathan and he said to him, "You son of a perverse and rebellious woman! Don't I know that you have sided with the son of Jesse to your own shame and to the shame of the mother who bore you? As long as the son of Jesse lives on this earth, neither you nor your kingdom will be established. Now send and bring him to me, for he must die!" "Why should he be put to death? What has he done?" Jonathan asked his father. But Saul hurled his spear at him to kill him. Then Jonathan knew that his father intended to kill David.

There are men and women who call themselves God's children who are not speaking to family, former friends or co-workers because they are angry. In times past they were hurt, but unlike cuts which heal, their wound festers-- constantly infected with the poison of displeasure and hostility. They lose precious time every day consumed with thoughts of getting revenge, of seeing those who hurt them punished.

Perhaps the object of their wrath is God. They feel betrayed, let down, smashed beneath the unfeeling, graceless existence of a brutal life. Where is God when needed?

King Saul, in the preceding passage, was consumed by jealousy and anger towards David. His anger was so fierce he tried to take his own son's life. Not only does unrighteous anger prevent us from thinking clearly it also causes us to disobey God's voice. The problem is our inability to control our emotions, our unwillingness to release to God whatever has hurt us. The difference between righteous anger and unrighteous anger is as distinct as the contrast between Rocky Mountain streams and Tennessee rivers.

Unrighteous anger comes in two forms. The first slowly heats over time. Paul wrote the Ephesians:

"In your anger do not sin": Do not let the sun go down while you are still angry, and do not give the devil a foothold . . . Get rid of all bitterness, rage and anger, brawling and slander, along with every form of malice (Eph.4:26,27,31).

Brooding anger is that which eats constantly at the heart of its host. Whether days or decades, the life of this anger gives the devil the ability to step in and rip apart the holy life God wants us to experience.

Rage, or flash anger is that which erupts suddenly and uncontrollably. It does not know the advice of Seneca— "The greatest remedy for anger is delay." It causes us to spew words we cannot take back or to blindly act in a treacherous manner as Saul did when he hurled his spear to kill his own son. James wrote:

My dear brothers, take note of this: Everyone should be quick to listen, slow to speak and slow to become angry, for man's anger does not bring about the righteous life that God desires (James 1:19,20).

Righteous anger (like Jesus demonstrated when cleansing the temple (John 4:15-17), is always under control and directed for the purpose of protecting God's reputation or furthering His will. It is rarely displayed and does not lead to sin.

If you are one who struggles with anger there is one clear solution. You must repent of your bottled hostility and confess to God the sin of refusing to trust Him by taking matters into your own hands. What perpetuates anger is our pride. We feel sorry for ourselves. We don't want to let go of claimed rights because we feel justified in our emotions. We want things to go our way. But if being right is the track and anger its train, we are steaming nowhere. Our focus must be on Christ not on who wronged us. Give it up. Let it go. Why let the devil be your conductor.

Inspiration

Whenever you are angry, be assured that it is not only a present evil, but that you have increased a habit.— Epictetus

Speak when you're angry--and you'll make the best speech you'll ever regret.—Laurence J. Peter

Anger is a fire; it catches, destroys, and consumes. Let us quench it by long-suffering and forbearance. For as red hot iron dipped into water loses its fire, so an angry man falling in with a patient one does no harm to the patient man, but rather benefits him and is himself more thoroughly subdued.— Chrysostom, in *Homilies on Hebrews*

All time spent angry is time lost being happy.— Mexican Proverb

COMPLACENCY

It was a cold evening on the high ground. I briefed my platoon sergeant and my orders were clear. Keep guards awake through the night. We were engaged in a field training exercise and could not afford to let the enemy breach our perimeter. Around 2:00 a.m. I awoke. Quietly I left my position to walk the line. All my men were asleep. Position by position I grabbed their M16's and M60 machine guns until I had every weapon I could snatch. Then I woke up my platoon sergeant and presented the arsenal to him. I watched in silence as he rousted every squad and ripped them for sleeping on duty.

Our Focus

Amos 6:1-7—Woe to you who are complacent in Zion, and to you who feel secure on Mount Samaria, you notable men of the foremost nation, to whom the people of Israel come! . . . You put off the evil day and bring near a reign of terror. You lie on beds inlaid with ivory and lounge on your couches. You dine on choice lambs and fattened calves. You strum away on your harps like David and improvise on musical instruments. You drink wine by the bowlful and use the finest lotions, but you do not grieve over the ruin of Joseph. Therefore you will be among the first to go into exile; your feasting and lounging will end.

I despise complacency. I've seen what it can do in my own life and the lives of those around me. It is one of the most sinister enemies we Christians face. It is like taking drugs in small doses until over time the buildup renders the user useless.

A complacent Christian is not aware enough of danger to care. His lack of vigilance threatens his buddies' lives as well as his own. Complacency says, "I don't need to exercise it's more fun to eat." "Don't tell me what to do, I like my life the way it is." Complacent Christians protect their passivity by being critical of others. They justify not taking action by finding fault in the action or inaction of others. Maintaining comfort becomes more important than truth itself. Just ask Peter. He thought Jesus was overly morbid. He assured Him of his love. Yet he fell asleep when Christ most needed his prayer support. He betrayed his Lord when identified as His follower. Maybe we ought to listen to this seasoned apostle when he poignantly writes:

Be self-controlled and alert. Your enemy the devil prowls around like a roaring lion looking for someone to devour. Resist him, standing firm in the faith, because you know that your brothers throughout the world are undergoing the same kind of sufferings (1 Pe.5:8,9).

Inspiration

Danger past, God forgotten.—Scottish Proverb

You cannot go on being a good egg forever. You must either hatch or rot.—C. S. Lewis

I would like to buy $3 worth of God, please, not enough to explode my soul or disturb my sleep but just enough to equal a cup of warm milk or a snooze in the sunshine. I don't want enough of him to make me love a black man or pick beets with a migrant. I want ecstasy, not transformation; I want the warmth of the womb, not a new birth. I want a pound of the Eternal in a paper sack. I would like to buy $3 worth of God, please.—Wilbur Rees

COMPLAINING

> ### Our Focus
>
> Numbers 14:1-4—That night all the people of the community raised their voices and wept aloud. All the Israelites grumbled against Moses and Aaron, and the whole assembly said to them, "If only we had died in Egypt! Or in this desert! Why is the Lord bringing us to this land only to let us fall by the sword? Our wives and children will be taken as plunder. Wouldn't it be better for us to go back to Egypt?" And they said to each other, "We should choose a leader and go back to Egypt."
>
> Philippians 2:14—Do everything without complaining or arguing.

What is the first question a child asks with increasing frequency on a long trip? "Daddy, are we almost there yet!" The first couple of times dad responds with dignity and grace. Then mom senses the repeating question becomes an irritant so she provides the answer. It wouldn't be so bad except the questions change in step with the child's demeanor. The whine level rises. Each succeeding statement has more bite. Note the progression!

Statement   (Translation)
How long 'til we get there?
(Man this trip is taking forever!)

I'm bored! Why can't we get out now?
(You are not providing me an exciting environment)

It's hot back here, my legs need more room.
(We need a bigger vehicle.)

Why did we have to bring so much stuff?
(You are insensitive to my spatial needs.)

I Keep Asking

She's kicking me!
(I don't like the company I have to sit by!)

I wish we'd stayed home. I want to go home!
(You are to blame, I should have been in charge.)

"Oh, the journey! Will I go bananas before this road trip ends or will I buy straightjackets for my kids!"

"Oh, this journey!" we say of life. Complaining start out innocently. It is the honest inquiry from eyes that canno see tomorrow and merely need reassurance. But when th environment is not to our liking, the odyssey become unpleasant. We begin to question God's leadership. "Ar You sure You know what You are doing?"

Oh, the journey! The road of life has potholes! Wh must we endure unexpected flats, blown transmission broken hoses and construction delays? Suffering was no part of our plan. With our changing perspective we ceas looking up to God. He is suddenly insensitive to our need Our adversity is His fault. "If only" becomes our *imbroglic* our twisted theme song. If we are not careful, the day wil come when our incessant complaints transcend into murmuring of mutiny—we want to go back to Egypt.

"Oh, the journey!" God says. "How long will I b patient with these children of Mine who question Me ever step of the way."

One has to wonder if the reason so many Christian leave ministry is directly related to the complaining spirit s prevalent among God's children. Complaining saps th strength of those serving. It poisons the spirit of those whos mouths reveal what their heart contains. Finally, it is subtl rebellion against God's authority.

Have you ever poured milk into a glass only to find a first taste that it is sour? Yeeech! Complaining is th evidence of a good spirit gone bad. Just as we wouldn' drink sour milk, so God will not fellowship with those of cantankerous spirit.

Inspiration

Complaining is the outward expression of discontent from within . . . Regardless of whatever circumstances may cause discontent or dissatisfaction, complaining is always an expression of unbelief toward God's order in our life.—Reverend Dale A. Robbins

We cannot look up if we are murmuring.—Oswald Chambers in *The Pilgrim's Song Book*

COVETING

Our Focus

2 Corinthians 8:9—You know how full of love and kindness our Lord Jesus Christ was. Though He was very rich, yet for your sakes He became poor, so that by His poverty He could make you rich. (NLT)

Rather incredible isn't it? The Lord of the universe willingly disrobed of the heavenly splendor that was His. He set aside His royal power to be mocked, slapped, spit on and spiked to a cross--put to death by the very people He came to save. He allowed Himself to be constrained by the limitations of a human body experiencing hunger, thirst, pain, fatigue and the incessant onslaught of temptation.

When the rich young ruler asked Jesus what good thing he should do to get eternal life Jesus said, **"If you want to be perfect, go, sell your possessions and give to the poor, and you will have treasure in heaven. Then come, follow me"** (Mat.19:21). When he turned away in sadness on account of his great wealth, he had no idea what splendor Jesus had set aside. No idea! He sadly walked away from the Savior Who left heaven and all its glory, to live on earth in all its sin.

What can we learn from the rich young ruler? Perhaps what we possess or want to possess, can literally become more important than wholeheartedly pursuing God. Despite this man's grasp of truth, he could not break free of the clutches of wealth. There are lots of things which if we covet and grasp too tightly, may hinder what God wants to do in our lives. Time, money, friends, possessions, sleep, leisure hours, sports, hobbies . . . the list runs on!

If the thought of setting aside anything to follow Jesus makes us defensive, the proof of our misplaced priorities is self-evident. Have we considered that the poverty Jesus embraced is the richness of our salvation?

Evan met the Lord at a concert after some friends shared with him the gospel. At first he was eager to fellowship with other Christians and to soak up all that he could about God. He faithfully came to church, served those around him with his talents and professed to see changes occurring in his life. But Evan had a problem. He had an insatiable appetite for toys. His wife, Jane, had a similar weakness. She could not stop buying clothes.

First, he needed a motorcycle. Jane wanted a jacuzzi. With each acquisition their credit card debt grew. Soon, fellowship stood in the way of his work. He had to take a second job just to pay the bills so he could keep his toys. He didn't have time to spend reading the Bible anymore. He was too tired. Ironically, he couldn't even enjoy his possessions—he was working too much.

Unfortunately, Evan and Jane are living for that which will burn. Nothing they buy will go to heaven. They will have to explain to God why they forsook Him. It is truly tragic how many couples are running hard to acquire whatever their eyes covet next. Jesus warned of the seed that was planted and grew only to be choked by thorns. Those thorns represent the worries of this life and the deceitfulness of wealth (Mat.13:22). What owns you?

Inspiration

There is nothing wrong with men possessing riches. The wrong comes when riches possess men.— Reverend Billy Graham

There is within the human heart a tough fibrous root of fallen life whose nature is to possess, always to possess. It covets "things" with a deep and fierce passion. The pronouns "my" and "mine" look innocent enough in print, but their constant and universal use is significant. They express the real nature of the old Adamic man better than a thousand volumes of theology could do. They are verbal symptoms of our deep disease. The roots of our hearts have grown down into *things*, and we dare not pull up one rootlet lest we die. Things have become necessary to us. . . God's gifts now take the place of God.—A.W. Tozer

The end of the twentieth century revealed in the United States a direct ratio between affluence and discontentment, i.e. the more we have, the more discontent we tend to be. Those who don't have as much as others have are envious.—Walt Henrichsen

Our Lord Jesus Christ became poor for our sakes not as an example, but to give us the unerring secret of His religion. Professional Christianity is a religion of possessions that are devoted to God; the religion of Jesus Christ is a religion of personal relationship to God, and has nothing whatever to do with possessions. The disciple is rich not in possessions, but in personal identity. Voluntary poverty was the marked condition of Jesus (Luke 9:58), and the poverty of God's children in all ages is a significant thing. Today we are ashamed and afraid to be poor.—Oswald Chambers in *Approved Unto God*

DEPRESSION

Our Focus

Psalm 88:2-7—May my prayer come before You; turn Your ear to my cry. For my soul is full of trouble and my life draws near the grave. I am counted among those who go down to the pit; I am like a man without strength. I am set apart with the dead, like the slain who lie in the grave, whom You remember no more, who are cut off from Your care. You have put me in the lowest pit, in the darkest depths. Your wrath lies heavily upon me; You have over-whelmed me with all Your waves.

She sits at home and stares out the window. The hours pass with little thought of significance for she has lost her way. Work, what can be done, lacks quality but she doesn't care. She finds tears where once there was laughter. She fears people she once strode among easily. Her thoughts betray her. Her body languishes yet with no explanation. She is depressed. Her forlorn cry is, "I don't care!"

According to a report put out by Hopkins Technology, "One-fourth of all women and one-eighth of all men will suffer at least one episode or occurrence of depression during their lifetimes." That's enough melancholy to fill an ocean. Depression, whether caused by a chemical imbalance, great loss, loneliness, unconfessed sin, or some tragic set-back, is not to be taken lightly.

We once had a man living in our home who suffered acute bouts of depression. When they came it was all he could do to go to work. Once he got home he went right to bed. He felt unloved and unlovely. We found that the voice of the enemy was quick to whisper that he was worthless. His standing before God was undermined by laying in a quagmire of self-doubt.

Depression is like leprosy. It eats away all that is good leaving its victim disfigured, an outcast among those adorned with joy. The worst advice to give to a person depressed is "Come on, snap out of it! Stop moping and get back to work." If it were that easy, no one would stay in the valley of gloom.

If you are depressed, seek help. Cry out to God and go after spiritual and if necessary, medical treatment. Just as a plant cannot grow without light, so a person immersed in darkness so thick it dampens all joy, will eventually wilt and wonder what happened to God. The first step to freedom is admitting the problem. While the Lord may test you, He will not withdraw His hand from you beyond what you can bear. So go after Him. He will hear your cry. Don't give up!

Definition

The signs of depression include sadness, apathy and inertia which makes it difficult to "get going" or to make decisions; loss of energy and fatigue which often are accompanied by insomnia; pessimism and hopelessness; fear; a negative self-concept often accompanied by self-criticism and feelings of guilt, shame, worthlessness and helplessness; a loss of interest in work, sex, and usual activities; a loss of spontaneity; difficulties in concentration; an inability to enjoy pleasurable events or activities; and often a loss of appetite . . . In many cases the symptoms of depression hide anger which has not been expressed, sometimes isn't recognized and—according to traditional psychiatric theory—is turned inward against oneself.—Gary R. Collins in *Christian Counseling*

Although depression is often thought of a being an extreme state of sadness, there is a vast difference between clinical depression and sadness. Sadness is a part of being human, a natural reaction to painful circumstances. All of us will experience sadness at some point in our lives. Depression, however, is a physical illness with many more symptoms than an unhappy mood . . . Depression can linger for weeks, months or even years. The sad person feels bad, but continues to cope with living. A person with clinical depression may feel overwhelmed and hopeless.—Nancy Schimelpfening

DISOBEDIENCE

Aber and I sat at the table and dipped the addicting chips in delicious hot sauce. Aber asked if we could meet. He was spiritually hungry, eager to learn more about God. After our usual chitchat, he shared about a vivacious gal at work on his team. She had recently moved to Oregon from Massachusetts. He noted her athleticism and that the two of them were working out three times a week during lunch. He was losing weight and felt great. The chips I'd been munching suddenly lost their flavor.

"Aber you're married. Do you think it is wise for you to be working out with this woman?" His answer was evasive. Red flags began flapping. I shared Pro.16:17—"**The highway of the upright avoids evil; he who guards his way guards his life**." We looked at Job 31:1—"**I made a covenant with my eyes not to look lustfully at a girl**." But Aber laughed at my concern. He was mildly offended at the implication that any evil might be involved. He said I was overreacting—after all they were just friends and he loved his wife and wouldn't do anything stupid.

Eight weeks later Aber could not look me in the eyes. He'd decided to separate from his wife. He rented an apartment, and in order to afford the cost, talked his workout partner into moving in with him. He swept over every move with a tightly twined broom of rationalism. His finishing touch was how excited he was at the opportunity to share about Christ with his new live-in. It was as if sharing God would somehow appease deliberate unfaithfulness.

Moses taught his people that following God meant obeying the commands He made for their own betterment (see Deu. 28). Jesus said, "**the world must learn that I love the Father and that I do <u>exactly</u> what My Father has commanded Me**" (John 14:31). Do we understand through what the Bible teaches that in following God's commands there is no room for deviation? We cannot wander into pornography. We cannot rationalize a homosexual relationship as right because it is a loving one or because we were born with an affinity for those of the same sex. We cannot gossip or stay angry, slander or gamble away money. What God forbids in His word, we are to keep as forbidden. The moment we create our own path aren't we, in effect, saying we know better than God does? The instant we rationalize aberrant behavior we cease to follow wholeheartedly our Father. We separate ourselves from His blessing.

We either do what God asks or we stray. Follow is not a wishy-washy word. Nor is it hard to find out what God wants. He has supplemented His commands by equipping us with a built-in conscience. Isn't selective compliance really a *euphemistic* form for rebellion? The Infantry says, "Lead, follow or get the hell out of the way." God says follow my lead and hell won't be in your way!

Our Focus

Deuteronomy 4:2—Do not add to what I command you and do not subtract from it, but keep the commands of the Lord your God that I give you.

2 Chronicles 24:20b--Why do you disobey the Lord's commands? You will not prosper. Because you have forsaken the LORD, he has forsaken you.

Psalm 7:14,15—He who is pregnant with evil and conceives trouble gives birth to disillusionment. He who digs a hole and scoops it out falls into the pit he has made.

John 14:23—Jesus replied, "If anyone loves Me, he will obey my teaching. My Father will love him, and we will come to him and make our home with him."

If we believe that we can assemble a life that is spiritually sound on the basis of our own insights, we are as naïve as a chicken wandering into a wolf's den. The key to building a strong spiritual life is not buried by God in the sand of common sense. Instead, recognizing our blinded state from sin, He makes His will wonderfully clear that if we want to be great and blessed in His kingdom, we must obey His word. Let's turn up our spiritual transistors to intercept a few excuses heaven hears from believers uninterested in becoming spiritually compliant.

Borice Busy: *"God is not here in my size 10 ½ Nikes. He doesn't understand that I don't have time to always do what He would like."* On the basis of such logic, Borice's spiritual pilgrimage is placed on hold by the competing calls of other interests. His foundation is based on rubber as he bounces from one activity to the next.

Trent Trendy: *"God's word was written by men over 19 centuries ago and beyond. His commands are wonderful but not relevant for where I am today."* Trent doesn't truly believe God's word is **"living and active, sharper than any double-edged sword, able to judge the thoughts and attitudes of the heart"** (Heb.4:12). In truth, he sees God as a relic and adorns his walls with antique pronouncements that look good on parchment. His true god is rationalization and his foundation is the slick clay of humanism.

Swendy Simple: *"God's word is too hard to comprehend. It's best if I just do that which makes sense."* If Swendy refused to heed the warning on the hair dryer cord because she didn't understand it, she would probably end up a crispy critter, electrocuted by plugging the wet cord into the wall socket. Just because we don't understand something doesn't mean we shouldn't obey. God asks us to follow His commands for perfect reasons.

Corky Quibble: *"It is impossible for me to do all that God asks—there is no way I can be perfect, so I might as well just do what comes naturally, after all He'll forgive me when I confess."*

Imagine a basketball player refusing to practice free throws because he can't make them shooting in a game! God expects us to strive to keep His instruction knowing we will benefit in the process.

You and I can live happy and fun-filled lives but if we are not anchored into obeying God's word, sin will eventually take us over the edge. Obedience isn't a dirty word. It's what makes us light to people locked in spiritual brownouts. So the next time, the Holy Spirit grabs your attention with divine instruction—do it! You'll not regret it—He guarantees it!

Inspiration

 When Norman Vincent Peale was a boy, he found a big, black cigar, slipped into an alley, and lit up. It didn't taste good, but it made him feel very grown up . . . until he saw his father coming. Quickly he put the cigar behind his back and tried to be casual. Desperate to divert his father's attention, Norman pointed to a billboard advertising the circus. "Can I go, Dad? Please, let's go when it comes to town." His father's reply taught Norman a lesson he never forgot. "Son," he answered quietly but firmly, "never make a petition while at the same time trying to hide a smoldering disobedience."—John Lavender in *Why Prayers Are Unanswered* as quoted by Kirk Russel, DeForest, Wisconsin. *Leadership*, Vol. 4, no. 4.

The golden rule for understanding in spiritual matters, is not intellect, but obedience . . . If a person wants scientific knowledge, intellectual curiosity is one's guide; but if a person wants insight into what Jesus Christ teaches, one can only get it by obedience. If things are dark to us spiritually, it is because there is something we will not do. Intellectual darkness comes because of ignorance; spiritual darkness comes because of something I do not intend to obey.—Oswald Chambers in *Studies in the Sermon on the Mount*

If God speaks and you hear but do not respond, a time could come when you will not hear His voice. Disobedience can lead to a "famine of hearing the words of the Lord" (Amos 8:11-12).—Henry T. Blackaby & Claude V. King in *Experiencing God*

DOGMATISM

If being right is most important, listening may be a lost cause.   There is a cost for preferring stubbornness to sensitivity, opinion to grace. For isn't it true that there still remain churches:

- Where a black man is not welcome in a white man's sanctuary.
- Who reject your baptism experience because you were not "dunked" by a doctrinally-correct (DC) clergyman.
- That only accept the King James Version otherwise you don't have the Word of God.
- Where drums, saxophones, guitars and trombones have no place because they are instruments of the devil.
- Where the preacher dare not exceed thirty minutes or the service has gone too long.
- Where the visitor had better not sit in Elmira's family pew.
- Split because a Calvinist will not worship with an Arminian or vice versa.
- That will not adequately pay their pastor because "God's servants should be humble (translation—controlled!).
- That will not share the good news for fear newcomers would "ruin" their already comfortable fellowship?

Our Focus

Jeremiah 7:24—But they did not listen or pay attention; instead, they followed the stubborn inclinations of their evil hearts. They went backward and not forward.

Dogmatism comes with a price. We remain critical of others. Law replaces love. Views take precedence over vision. Rather than focus on growing in godliness we become centered on chapter and verse. The world of course sees all this with the result that our dogmatism is a great stumbling block. Consequently, we will stand accountable before God for hindering people from finding His Son.

Occasionally I receive letters from someone bent on proving that the only Biblical translation people should be using is the Authorized or King James Version. This person is consumed with being right but at what cost? Somehow I don't believe the angels are sitting in heaven moaning because people have left the KJV to use a modern version.

When we focus our attention on God, He rewards us by giving us the wisdom to understand what cannot be compromised versus what is nonessential. We discover that what is paramount is not how strongly we cling to our views but how well we know our Lord! Are you afraid to be wrong? Is that fear coming from the Lord or from pride? The former instills discernment with humility while the latter produces stubbornness and a brittle demeanor.

Inspiration

The further we get away from Jesus the more dogmatic we become over what we call our religious beliefs, while the nearer we live to Jesus the less we have of certitude and the more of confidence in Him.—Oswald Chambers in *Disciples Indeed*

If a given translation - any translation - is to be "better" than another, it should therefore lead those who use it to a fuller experience with the Lord Jesus Christ. Their lives should exhibit more Christlike (sic) behavior, as a whole, than believers who use other "less correct" versions. Sadly, this has not been the case. There is a group, I am almost tempted to call them a cult, that exalts the 1611 KJV to a level I would almost call worship.—http://www.mindspring.com/~brucec/hypocrites.htm

FEAR

Jenny's boss hit her one day—hard enough to put her in tears but not hard enough to leave a bruise. When no one else was in the office he mocked her and demeaned her work. She wouldn't say anything to him unless it was a plea for him to stop. She was too afraid to go for help for fear she would lose her job. Jenny is a wonderful gal. Unless you were perceptive you might not know that inside her run the twisted and frayed nerves of a fearful woman.

Our Focus

Psalm 23:4—Even though I walk through the valley of the shadow of death, I will fear no evil, for You are with me; Your rod and Your staff, they comfort me.

Psalm 27:1—The Lord is my light and my salvation—whom shall I fear? The Lord is the stronghold of my life—of whom shall I be afraid?

Romans 8:15—For you did not receive a spirit that makes you a slave again to fear, but you received the Spirit of sonship. And by Him we cry, "Abba, Father."

Fear is often a dwarf masquerading in giant's clothing. Whether real or imagined it can be an insurmountable obstacle to our spiritual growth. The New Testament offers us several examples of this. Jesus healed a man who called himself Legion because many demons had gone into him. When the people in the region of the Gerasenes heard of his healing and how a herd of pigs feeding nearby ran madly off a steep bank into the lake and drowned, they begged Jesus to leave because they were overcome with fear. Rather than trust this Son of Man Who mightily freed a man in bondage, they focused on out-of-control pigs and the discomfort of an insane man now walking about in his right mind (Luke 8:26-

37).

The Apostle John tells us that many Jewish leaders believed in Jesus but they would not follow Him for fear that the Pharisees would throw them out of the synagogue (John 12:42). They sacrificed truth on their own altar of prestige and social acceptance.

The causes of fear are the cancers of faith. I don't want to lose something. I am afraid harm will come to me. So I give in to what paralyzes my ability to grow and become a prisoner in my own body. When we place our confidence in Jesus, we our freed from the spirit of fear. We become children of God sheltered under the arms of our omnipotent Father. We see what this looks like in the boldness of the Apostles who were not afraid to lose their lives spreading the gospel because they believed that Christ truly was their Savior. When He rose from the dead, their fears were given a proper burial.

To live in fear is to believe that God is not able, a grotesque lie of Lucifer. To cower is to dance to the shake of rattled bones instead of gyrating to the praise of a redeemed spirit. Don't be impaled by the spear of fear. Be like King David who wrote, "**I sought the Lord, and He answered me; he delivered me from all my fears**" (Psa.34:4).

Inspiration

The fierce grip of panic need not immobilize you. God knows no limitation when it comes to deliverance. Admit your fear. Commit it to Him. Dump the pressure on Him; He can handle it.— Pastor Charles Swindoll in *three steps forward two steps back*

Anxiety is the secret wound of modern man.— Helmut Thielicke in *The Silence Of God*

GUILT

Judy called Elaine to invite her to First Baptist's famous women's retreat. Elaine wouldn't go. Although her calendar was clear her mind was clouded so she begged off. As badly as she wanted to be there with the other women for what she knew would be dynamic fellowship—she felt unworthy.

Five years before, Elaine had an affair. She'd innocently started working out at lunch with a co-worker, a guy with a great personality. Remember Aber? She rationalized her time with him until what first just met emotional needs turned physical. Naturally, when the sin was uncovered, her husband was devastated. He determined to stay with her and make the marriage work even after she had moved out. She agreed to go with him to counseling. Their church had rallied behind them. But it was too much. She couldn't fellowship with her old friends, convinced they secretly looked down on her. So they'd settled on a new church. But now, when she should be growing in her love with God, she found herself stuck.

Our Focus

Psalm 38:4—My guilt has overwhelmed me like a burden too heavy to bear.

Psalm 69:5—You know my folly, O God; my guilt is not hidden from You.

Have you ever had a back or headache that just wouldn't go away? That is what carrying around guilt is like. No matter what we are experiencing, the nagging weight of some wrong we've committed won't be shaken loose.

There are two kinds of guilt. The first type is caused by unconfessed sin. Whenever we knowingly break God's commandments and then hide what we've done guilt takes residence in our heart. With sin and guilt in our life, our

I Keep Asking

relationship with God is damaged. The tragedy of unconfessed sin is that God knows what we've done. Nothing we do or think escapes His attention. Hiding sin only results in our being miserable. It makes us subservient to our own unhealthy pride. Don't believe the lie that guilt will just go away! Ask the woman who aborted her baby. Query the man who stole from his company. Search your own heart—have you engaged in wrongdoing at no cost?

The second type of guilt is caused by unbelief. It occurs when a believer commits a wrong, confesses before God and repents of the evil done but cannot shake a sense that the crime is too big for God to forgive. Many Christians like Elaine in the fictitious story above, are sorry for their sin and have asked God to forgive them. They just don't believe He really has. They cannot take their eyes off themselves and focus on Jesus. Of course, Satan is a huge fan of keeping people enslaved to guilty feelings. He would have us stay mired in a sense of unworthiness, caught in our own pity.

If we would read and believe Heb.10:19-23, we would find God's remedy to our guilt.

Therefore, brothers, since we have confidence to enter the Most Holy Place by the blood of Jesus, by a new and living way opened for us through the curtain, that is, His body, and since we have a great Priest over the house of God, let us draw near to God with a sincere heart in full assurance of faith, having our hearts sprinkled to cleanse us from a guilty conscience and having our bodies washed with pure water. Let us hold unswervingly to the hope we profess, for He Who promised is faithful.

Jesus, by His shed blood absolved our sins—all of them. **"As far as the east is from the west, so far has He removed our transgressions from us"** (Psa.103:12). We don't have to carry around guilt. **"If we confess our sins, He**

106

is faithful and just and will forgive us our sins and purify us from all unrighteousness" (1 Jn.1:9).

To avoid fellowship because of sins of the past is to refuse to let Jesus forgive us! Don't let guilt master you. Let it go! Believe that God loves you. Then in faith you can move forward with Him leading the way!

Definition

 Guilt is so prevalent in our society that several types have been identified. These can be divided into two categories: objective guilt and subjective guilt. Objective guilt exists apart from our feelings. It occurs when a law has been broken and the lawbreaker is guilty even though he or she may not feel guilty. Subjective guilt refers to the inner feeling of remorse and self-condemnation which comes because of our actions.—Dr. Gary R. Collins in *Christian Counseling*

Even when suppressed, however, the knowledge of guilt always produces certain objective needs, which make their own demand for satisfaction irrespective of the state of the feelings. These needs include confession, atonement, reconciliation, and justification.—J. Budziszewski in *The Revenge of Conscience*

IMPULSIVENESS

Our Focus

Judges 11:30,31—And Jephthah made a vow to the Lord: "If You give the Ammonites into my hands, whatever comes out of the door of my house to meet me when I return in triumph from the Ammonites will be the Lord's, and I will sacrifice it as a burnt offering."

It is one of the most bizarre stories in the Bible. Jephthah, the Gileadite was a mighty warrior. His mother was a prostitute. His stepbrothers drove him away from home. So he settled in a place called Tob where a group of adventurers banded around him making him their leader. His prowess as a commander must have gained attention. Later when the Israelites were fighting the Ammonites, the same people who expelled him came and asked him to be their general.

Jephthah desperately wanted to defeat the Ammonites. So he uttered the vow recorded above. After the Lord brought victory to Israel and Jephthah returned home, who do you suppose came out of his home to greet him—his daughter—his only child. She came out dancing to tambourines for her triumphant dad. He tore his clothes in misery for a wretched vow to the Lord he could not break.

I don't understand why God or Jephthah's friends didn't stop him from sacrificing his daughter—a question for heaven. What I do understand is that his impulsive action was totally unnecessary. The Spirit of the Lord had already come upon him. God did not need a sacrificial vow to bring victory to His people. In his enthusiasm to win, this man made a horrible covenant.

Obstacles to Growth

I frequently observe people making impulsive decisions. I remember the time I first bought a car. I couldn't wait to have "wheels". I also wanted to impress those around me with my frugality by purchasing a very inexpensive car. So without doing much research, I went out and bought a Chevette. It was a poor decision. Later I traded it in for a Ford Ranger. I just had to have a truck. But that too, was an impulsive decision. Finally, after marrying Kathleen—who is tremendous at making wise purchases, we traded in the pickup for a reliable Suburu wagon. I could have saved thousands of dollars had I not been so impulsive.

Perhaps the two most obvious ways in which we reveal impulsiveness is how we use our money and our time. Life is short. God is great. We ought to act responsibly and with patience before we commit to making decisions that we will later regret. It is a sad thing to hear people start a sentence with the two words "If only . . ."

Make no excuses for impulsiveness—it is not a godly trait but rather a revealer of a character defect. Acting on impulse betrays a lack of trust in God, impatience, an "I want it now" selfishness, and a disregard for the future fallout of a present decision. Is not the way to glorify God through thoughtfulness, through a discerning and wise heart? Before making a hasty decision, why not identify a person you know to be wise and seek counsel! Turn to the Lord in prayer! May God help us to be wise for His glory and our peace.

Inspiration

The spiritual life is not impulsive; we are impulsive when we are not spiritual.—Oswald Chambers in *God's Workmanship*

Make haste slowly.—Suetonius

LAZINESS/CARELESSNESS

> To do nothing is in every man's power.
> —Samuel Johnson

"Reeenk, reeenk, reeenk! Reeenk, reeenk reeenk!" Shut that thing off—the obnoxious alarm—that dreaded voice of shrill reason. Hank knows his moment has come to rise. His plan was to read in Proverbs and Acts this morning and to pray before jumping in his Honda Prelude and scooting off to work. But his heart cry of conviction is silenced by the rapid motion of his left hand. "I'll just snooze a few more minutes then I'll get up."

Later, a bolt of thought shoots across his brain. "Oh no! I'm going to be late!" His feet flip off warm covers. With a rapid turning movement of an unbalanced body trying to wake up, he moves to the bathroom. A chain of events is now set in motion. God had a great word for Hank about patience from Solomon he will miss. At the office, he will react with anger to a critical comment from a colleague. His frustrated reply will sting, causing embarrassment--creating a need to repair a severed relationship.

Spiritually unfortified, Hank's perspective toward work, people and himself is jaded. When Jill calls to ask if he remembered to pray for her doctor's appointment, he says "yes" when in fact he forgot. As he hangs up, he throws up a quick prayer, "Lord help Jill, You know what she needs." Then he rationalizes his untruth—he didn't want to hurt her feelings. His shoulders sag.

Lunch was supposed to be with his accountability partner Phil. But yesterday, he got into an hour-long political debate with Jerry when he should have worked on his assigned project. Today, behind a pressing deadline, he calls to cancel with Phil. Little does he know that Phil is discouraged—wondering if he is unfit to help because not much seems to be working with Hank. At the end of the day, Hank will look back bemoaning his mistakes while he again stays up past midnight glued to the new computer racing game he bought.

> Proverbs 6:9-11—How long will you lie there, you sluggard? When will you get up from your sleep? A little sleep, a little slumber, a little folding of the hands to rest—and poverty will come on you like a vagrant and scarcity like a beggar.

We often think of laziness as too-much swing time on the favorite hammock. But laziness is not just an overindulgent sleep pattern. It can also be a habitual setting aside of any activity or work that should be accomplished. Instead of doing what we know is right we settle for what is fun or convenient. Laziness was never built on beams of bad intentions. But every piece of *indolence* is warped and results in a finished product devoid of the sheen and substance God intended. The sad line of sloth is always, "I deserve this break." And break is what indeed happens. For lack of discipline feeds an unmotivated spirit. Are you swayed by those thoughts that resist discipline? If so, resolve to get serious. Don't let your love for God be usurped by idleness or choosing questionable activity.

Inspiration/Definition

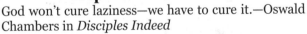

God won't cure laziness—we have to cure it.—Oswald Chambers in *Disciples Indeed*

Sloth is more than indolence and physical laziness. In fact, it can reveal itself in frenetic activism as easily as in lethargy because its roots are spiritual rather than physical. It is a condition of explicitly spiritual dejection that has given up on the pursuit of God, the true, the good, and the beautiful. Sloth is inner despair at the worthwhileness of the worthwhile that finally slumps into an attitude of "Who cares?"--Os Guiness in *The Call*

LEGALISM

> Some men die by shrapnel,
> Some go down in flames.
> But most men perish inch by inch
> playing little games.—Unknown

Orthodox Jews understand that 39 kinds of work are forbidden on the Sabbath under prevailing *Halakah*. The religious party called Pharisees were experts in the law. Today we would consider them legalists. We recognize them as the black and white thinkers among our friends, co-workers and relatives. In fact we ourselves may be wired as such. Every society needs law-proponents. But if taken to the extreme, legalism may spawn five serious problems.

1. **Legalism is burdensome and a joy-killer.** When Jesus offered to give rest to those weary and burdened in Mat.11:28, part of the load the people were carrying was trying to live up to a multitude of laws. For example the Jewish Mishna in M. Hagigah 1:8 says, "the rules about the Sabbath . . . are as mountains hanging by a hair, for [teaching of] Scripture [thereon] is scanty and the rules many". I don't know about you, but whenever I am around unbalanced legalists I find my joy sapped by the ever-flowing stream of attention to the nit nat and nit noid.

2. **Legalism draws attention to its possessor.** Jesus said of the religious leaders:

> **Everything they do is for show. On their arms they wear extra wide prayer boxes with Scripture verses inside, and they wear extra long tassels on their robes. And how they love to sit at the head table at banquets and in the most prominent seats in the synagogue! They enjoy the attention they get on the streets, and they enjoy being called 'Rabbi'** (Mat.23:5-7 NLT).

3. Legalism preserves the tree at the expense of the forest. "It is the spirit and not the form of law that keeps justice alive" wrote Earl Warren. Those who focus on the letter of the law often miss the intent for which the law originated.

4. Legalism is often symptomatic of a deeper issue: jealousy, insecurity, fear, unbelief.

> In my opinion, unbelief is the root cause of all legalism. How? It refuses to accept God's covenant promises—that His Spirit will subdue our sins, empower us to obey, instill His fear in us, cause us to walk uprightly, give us a hatred for sin. When we depart from the truth of God's covenant, no longer trusting and waiting on Him to do the work, we turn to legalism. We construct our own set of rigid rules devoid of the Spirit's power—David Wilkerson.

5. Legalism is often fraught with muddy thinking and double standards. After Jesus healed the man's shriveled hand in the synagogue, the Pharisees went out and plotted to kill Him. How could men passionate to preserve the Sabbath conspire to murder?! They were not simply infuriated by Jesus breaking Sabbath rules. They were angry because of His claims of authority (Mat.12:6,8). Jesus taught:

> **The teachers of the law and the Pharisees sit in Moses' seat. So you must obey them and do everything they tell you. But do not do what they do, for they do not practice what they preach. They tie up heavy loads and put them on men's shoulders, but they themselves are not willing to lift a finger to move them . . . The greatest among you will be your servant** (Mat. 23:2-4, 11).

Does this mean we have the freedom to chuck the law or think less of legalists? No! For Jesus said, "**Do not think that I have come to abolish the Law or the Prophets; I**

113

have not come to abolish them but to fulfill them" (Mat. 5:17). The challenge we face is to uphold God's laws while maintaining a careful understanding of the intent and application of them. If we are more consumed with keeping the law than in loving God and our fellowman, we are in jeopardy of actually turning people away from God's glorious kingdom!

Our Focus

Matthew 12:9-12—Going on from that place, He went into their synagogue, and a man with a shriveled hand was there. Looking for a reason to accuse Jesus, they asked Him, "Is it lawful to heal on the Sabbath?" He said to them, "If any of you has a sheep and it falls into a pit on the Sabbath, will you not take hold of it and lift it out? How much more valuable is a man than a sheep! Therefore it is lawful to do good on the Sabbath."

I know a man who sees everything black or white. Maybe you know him too. He is zealous for the truth. He is a defender of justice who confidently speaks for God. His critical eye is the first to spot error in others and in himself. He is meticulous in his theology, mastered in the school of answers, mindful of all the rules.

This same man breaks fellowship with those who are inconsistent in their behavior. He is quick to list and condemn others' faults. He inhales rules while exhaling legalism. He fathoms justice but cannot swallow mercy. He eloquently recites chapter and verse but knows not the melody of God's sweet grace. Somewhere along his journey he veered from worshiping God to polishing the plaques proclaiming his intellectual prowess.

How can this man be so right and yet so full of error? Easy—cease focusing on God and insist on protecting His laws and see what happens. Jesus blasted an entire religious group for their religious hypocrisy. They built and designed

Law subdivisions with well-articulated zoning instructions but were clueless towards the Law-Designer's intent. Ah, but let's not bash the Pharisees—we are all just as easily culpable. Anyone who values being right above knowing God is vulnerable to error. Note: Jesus never claimed exclusive office space in the Temple. He opened the Holy of Holies to a land desperate for salvation. He lived among the misguided. There might be a lesson we can learn from Him!

One can easily proclaim God's word and yet turn away God. Right living is not the key to God's truth. God's truth is the key to right living.

Inspiration

Legalists may have the right words but they don't know the music.—Author Unknown

Legalism wrenches the joy of the Lord from the Christian believer, and with the joy of the Lord goes his power for vital worship and vibrant service. Nothing is left but cramped, somber, dull and listless profession. The truth is betrayed, and the glorious name of the Lord becomes a synonym for a gloomy kill-joy. The Christian under law is a miserable parody of the real thing.—S. Lewis Johnson, Jr.

When I disassociate myself from God, I become a law to myself, and the first thing that happens is I don't love my neighbor as myself—I am so sure I am right and everyone else is wrong.— Oswald Chambers in *God's Workmanship*

LUST

Our Focus

Proverbs 6:25—Do not lust in your heart after her beauty or let her captivate you with her eyes.

A leopard ambushes its victims by staying camouflaged and it is so strong it can carry its prey high into a tree where other animals cannot steal it. Metaphorically, let us think of the leopard as a representative of lust.

Lust, like the cat always looking for prey, is never satisfied. I can have everything a person could want and still lust. Look at King David. At the height of his reign, with beautiful wives, immense popularity and power, all the food and wealth a man could need and he could not keep his eyes off Bathsheba. He had to have her. Today it's no different. You and I can instantly think of a well-known Christian supposedly at the top of his ministry caught living in adultery. And don't think lust is confined to sexual longings. It can hunger for money, possessions, power and prestige.

Lust lurks just off the main trail, always watching. We may go through wonderful times of spiritual growth but we dare not ever let our guard down lest we give in to our unrighteous desire. Unlike some of the more obvious obstacles to spiritual growth that we have examined, lust like the leopard, remains well hidden. I can sit in the middle of a worship service and have lustful thoughts of which no one around me is aware. And so can you.

Lust works best in the dark. It prefers to operate out of sight. However, sooner or later even those who cleverly engage in it are exposed. For those who are immersed in pornography or sexual escapades, you will find a waning zeal for worship, a lack of spiritual accountability, language that becomes less edifying, and a resistance to safeguards.

Lust is self-protective. Those who let lust have its way are masters of rationalization.

♦ "Oh, I don't need to obtain a filtered internet provider—I just stay away from questionable websites."

♦ "I see nothing wrong with meeting a member of the opposite sex privately!"

♦ "I can rent adult videos! People do it all the time and what I do in my home is my own business."

♦ "My spouse is not meeting my needs. What I do for fun so long as it is kept secret, is okay. God understands. Besides, I might have the opportunity to share the gospel with this other person."

♦ "You don't understand. You are just being judgmental, and a prude. Wake up, it's the 21st century."

Left unchecked, lust results in a string of tragedies. How many marriages will be ruined? How many people will be infected with embarrassing diseases? How many children will grow up confused, angry and bitter because of their parents unfaithfulness?

Hollywood has glorified lust as normal and fun. Yet those who run with *concupiscence* always end up disgusted with life, dissatisfied with God. Ironically, even the pleasure kingdom of Southern California has a way of revealing on the big screen the turmoil and heartache that results from cheating, obsessing and defrauding.

Jesus said if a man lusted in his heart for a woman, he had already committed adultery. He said this because He knew that adultery never begins in bed but rather in the heart. We ought to take heed to His warning.

Lust like every other spiritual obstacle can be overcome. The secret is to "just say NO!" Paul wrote the Corinthian Christians, **"We demolish arguments and every pretension that sets itself up against the knowledge of God, and we take captive <u>every</u> thought to make it obedient to Christ"** (2 Co.10:5). Paul was either a good liar or he was passing on to us valuable spiritual insight. Disobedient fascinations can be conquered with God's help—Php.4:13.

Don't allow yourself to become unaccountable to other believers. Don't go where you know you are unsafe. Don't think it makes you somehow weak to ask for help from others. Find someone (of the same sex!) you trust and weekly (daily if needed), make yourself accountable for your thoughts and actions. God will not share residency with a *prurient* priest. It's time for the priesthood of believers to declare a holy fast and starve the claw-clinging, fur-raising, hiss-producing, legion-growing, monsters of lust!

Inspiration

When I lust after a woman, I do violence to her dignity by failing to see her as a whole person and respect her as an image bearer of our God.—Adam R. Holz in "Letting Go of Lust", *Discipleship Journal* Issue 116

HE IS GRIEVED OVER THE SUDDEN MORAL BREAKDOWN OF THOSE WHO CALL THEMSELVES CHRISTIANS! That's right—in millions of Christian homes, so-called normal, godly people sit before cable TV or a VCR and drink in filthy, shameful, R-and X-rated movies. I believe I'm speaking to literally hundreds of thousands of Christians who are involved in such filth.—David Wilkerson in *America's Last Call*

NECROMANCY

Highway 58 in Virginia is a beautiful four-lane road that eventually ends in the Norfolk, Virginia Beach area. Tiny towns like Edgerton and Capron straddle the road. My family crossed through a great number of small communities in our adventure across America. It's absolutely amazing how many First Baptist Churches exist! Unfortunately it's even more amazing how many neon signs beckon customers to have their palms read.

Evidently, the practice of analyzing lines across hands is alive and well. I only hope that palms that open before the soothsayer are not the same that fold in prayer to an unseen Father. For God's people the operative word should be faith—trust that though I do not know what will come tomorrow, I am confident in the leading of the One Who made time. We walk by faith not by sight. If we think it is a harmless act of curiosity to consult a soothsayer or channel a spirit, we, in actuality, are rebelling against the Lord Who commanded, **"Do not turn to mediums or seek out spiritists, for you will be defiled by them. I am the Lord your God"** (Leviticus 19:31).

In the Old Testament, mediums were to be put to death by the Israelites. Does that sound unbelievably harsh? Well consider that these people were consulting spirits—not the Holy Spirit. They were setting themselves up in league with Satan to access information regarding the future—a total act of rebellion. Light cannot work in cooperation with the dark to shed new light. Is God's primary concern for us that we know tomorrow's outcome or that we live obediently today? What fuels those who consult spirits—is it perhaps fear, distrust and insecurity? What marks God's children—should it not be love, peace and abiding hope?

Our Focus

1 Samuel 28:8—So Saul disguised himself, putting on other clothes, and at night he and two men went to the woman. "Consult a spirit for me," he said, "and bring up for me the one I name."

The Bible tells the sad story in I Samuel of King Saul in desperation seeking the help of a witch to determine the outcome of a battle he faced. His broken relationship with God led him to disobey his own edict and consult a medium. Do not play with the toys of the occultist—those who deal in secrets. Do not embrace the dead to understand the living. To do so is to play with unholy fire.

Often today on television fortune tellers will advertise 1-900 numbers you can access to have your fortune revealed. Whether these folks are fakes is irrelevant. What you are being tempted to do sets you up to become a victim of the occult and a target of demons. God is completely clear in His Word that such activity is strictly off-limits.

Inspiration

If we turn to necromancy even in such seemingly ridiculous ways of telling fortunes in teacups or by cards or *planchette*, we commit a crime against our own souls, we are probing where we have no right to probe. People say, "There's no harm in it." There is all the harm and the backing of the devil in it. The only One who can open up the profound mysteries of life is God, and He will do it as He sees we can stand it.—Oswald Chambers in *The Servant as His Lord*

It is a grievous offense in the eyes of God for anyone to turn from His revealed Word to those who profess to have power to summon the spirits of the departed in order to give light and help. Such are either charlatans deceiving those who go to them or else possessed by impersonating demons misleading all who follow them.—Dr. H.A. Ironside

OPPRESSION

Her eyes turned from a beautiful blue hue to a steely gray. With the change in eye color came a different personality. Kindness, politeness, an attentive presence yielded to sarcasm, scorn and a confidence that seemed to reach across the table and suck out my strength. After what seemed like hours of trying to reason with her, I went back to my room completely exhausted. It was if I'd just finished running a 10KM race. I felt thoroughly defeated.

She was a great gal, a classmate of mine who decided to follow Christ as a junior the previous semester. During our summer vacation she was lonely and hungry to grow in her new found walk with Jesus. Unfortunately, she got mixed up with a group known as the Moonies. In New York, the Unification Church seems to have a lot of zoned-out followers of a *dissembling* Korean messiah.

Our Focus

Psalm 27:11—Teach me Your way, O Lord; lead me in a straight path because of my oppressors.

2 Corinthians 12:7-9—To keep me from becoming conceited because of these surpassingly great revelations, there was given me a thorn in my flesh, a messenger of Satan, to torment me. Three times I pleaded with the Lord to take it away from me. But He said to me, "My grace is sufficient for you, for My power is made perfect in weakness." Therefore I will boast all the more gladly about my weaknesses, so that Christ's power may rest on me.

1 Thessalonians 2:18—For we wanted to come to you--certainly I, Paul, did, again and again--but Satan stopped us.

I Keep Asking

I knew next to nothing about demon-oppression. I did my best to help Abigal* and basically got whacked by an unseen enemy far more cunning than I understood. Later, a younger member of our ministry team waded in to rescue her. He naively followed her to a retreat and came back a Moonie. As he resigned from the Military Academy to go to England in bondage to a crazy cult, we all got a sober dose of what the enemy was capable of doing.

There are three types of spiritual oppression. The first exists when we place ourselves in jeopardy by our sinful activity or communion with those involved in sinful activity. The second exists when people see our walk with God as a threat and do all they can to harm us. The third exists when Satan with God's permission, is allowed to directly afflict us as is illustrated in the middle passage of the Focus verses shown on the preceding page.

Spiritual oppression is deadly because Satan plays for our destruction. In America I believe the devil disguises his manipulation so most believers do not recognize his handiwork. Many doubt his existence. Had I not grown up in different countries in Asia and seen firsthand the spiritual bondage people live under I, too, would probably laugh at the notion of Satan working to crush Christians. In Southeast Asia, one can almost visibly feel the oppressive forces of darkness fed by hundreds of millions of people who bow to spirits, build shrines to tree gods, and worship Buddha with a fervor that would put many Christians to shame. I'm not laughing. And you shouldn't be either.

Satan often attacks Christians whose service to God is damaging to his kingdom. Anytime we walk with God we are subject to being oppressed. But if you indulge in pornography, take illegal drugs or engage in other conduct the Bible forbids, you are inviting the dominating influence of demons. I know too many families that allow their children to engage in unlawful behavior, for any number of reasons and consequently are physically, emotionally and spiritually oppressed and incapable of growing closer to God despite the fact that they maintain fellowship with other believers. Sadly, any fellowship or church body that refuses to deal with sin becomes divided and sickly (1 Co.5:1-5).

God does not fellowship where wickedness is permitted to thrive. He will not bring peace and victory to those who refuse to root out evil. He will not deliver those intent on rebelling. It breaks my heart. There is nothing worse than watching people you love live defeated before a ruthless enemy. But deliverance from oppression can only come when there is repentance, not rationalizing, not making lame excuses, and not avoiding necessary confrontation.

True love means standing in the authority of Jesus' name. Caution! This does not mean we should go out and seeing demons behind every bush, start commanding demons to flee. Our greatest task is not to worry about what Satan is doing. Rather, we are to focus on walking in obedience to God's commands. If we will walk in obedience to Him He will take care of us through His sovereign power. Our enemy can only do what God allows. The power of darkness is great but it cannot stand in the presence of His light.

If you are in the midst of feeling oppressed don't lose heart! Remember Who your Champion is! Eventually, even if you lose your life, if your heart is for Jesus, you will gain the eternal victory!

The Lord is a refuge for the oppressed, a stronghold in times of trouble. Those who know Your name will trust in You, for You, Lord, have never forsaken those who seek You" (Psa.9:9,10).

*Not her real name

Inspiration

When the Letter to the Hebrews declares that "we do not have a High Priest Who cannot sympathize with our weaknesses," it is reminding us that our Savior was subjected to a temptation that was real. Jesus felt the force of the assault of Satan in the very depths of His humanity.—RC Sproul in *The Glory of Christ*

Opposition is a fact: the Christian who is not conscious of being opposed had better watch himself for he is in danger. — J. I. Packer in *Knowing God*

Fall down seven times, get up eight.—Japanese Proverb

PREJUDICE

Nowhere in the Old Testament does it say love your neighbor and hate your enemies. So why did Jesus say, "You have heard that it was said . . ." (Mat.5:43)? At some point in time, zealous Jewish religious leaders made a mental leap of logic. They assumed that if they were to love their neighbor then the natural conclusion was animosity toward foreigners. While Christ walked in Israel, the prevailing spin on Lev.19:18 was that hatred of enemies was an acceptable and welcome thing.

Yet before we condemn the Pharisee we must examine our own track record. White men don hoods and in the name of Christ persecute black men. In the name of doctrine, believers have split into camps that spew venom toward one other. Unbelievers, already rife with prejudice, see no validity in Christianity. How can they when they see hatred alive in our very midst?

Jesus jolted His countrymen with the electric cry to love their enemies. He corrected their misconception of God by showing them His Father loves everyone. Would to God we might feel that same passion Jesus preached! One cannot be prejudiced and extend arms of righteousness. The authentic mark of the child of God is love. Without love we make a mockery of the Almighty! If anyone had the right to be prejudiced, it was God towards us and yet in His great love He sent Jesus to die for an earth full of rebellious children.

Prejudice is more than abnormal pride it is ignorance. One cannot camp in the supernatural light of God's presence and hate anyone.

I had the privilege once of meeting John Perkins, an eloquent preacher from Mississippi. John champions racial reconciliation despite the fact he was savagely beaten by white men bent on teaching this "uppity-nigger" a lesson; despite the pain of holding his dying brother in his arms--shot by a bigoted policeman. Why does John preach reconciliation? Because he came to understand God's love. A bitter man became a better man. A bitter land becomes a better land when we determine in our hearts that we will obey Jesus and let our light shine before men, that they may see our good deeds and praise our Father in heaven (Mat.5:16).

Our Focus

James 2:1-4—My brothers, as believers in our glorious Lord Jesus Christ, don't show favoritism. Suppose a man comes into your meeting wearing a gold ring and fine clothes, and a poor man in shabby clothes also comes in. If you show special attention to the man wearing fine clothes and say, "Here's a good seat for you," but say to the poor man, "You stand there" or "Sit on the floor by my feet," have you not discriminated among yourselves and become judges with evil thoughts?

Inspiration

Racism isn't a bad habit; it's not a mistake; it's a sin. The answer is not sociology; it's theology.—Pastor Anthony Evans

Carefully meditate on the following incident from the life of Mahatma Ghandi. This man, who later gained world attention, says in his autobiography that in his student days he was truly interested in the Bible. Deeply touched by reading the gospels, he seriously considered becoming a convert. Christianity seemed to offer the real solution to the caste system that was dividing the people of India. One Sunday he went to a nearby church to attend services. He decided to see the minister and ask for instruction in the way of salvation and enlightenment on other doctrines. But when he entered the sanctuary, the ushers refused to give him a seat and suggested that he go and worship with his own people. He left and never came back. "If Christians have caste differences also," he said to himself, "I might as well remain a Hindu." Believer, weed from your heart the evil root of intolerance before it yields the same bitter fruit.—Dr. James McCullen

REBELLING

Rebellion runs in the human family. It is part of our sinful nature.—Pastor John Piper

I wonder if every church has them. Their profile is not hard to spot. They wear the cloth of disenchantment with authority. They chaff at rules or the appearance of any type of rigidity. They love to question the motives of those who make decisions. They take pride if the crowd goes left, in going right. They wear their stubbornness as a badge of courage and refuse to bend. Don't ever tell them they <u>must</u> do something for the word "must" is a dirty word.

While it would appear that they struggle with authority, it is the sovereignty of God which really trips them up and for good reason. Generally rebels are those who have suffered at the hands of tyrants while growing up. They have learned by being burned to recognize and detest poor leadership, to be suspicious of those who possess real or perceived power. Since God ultimately allowed them to suffer under the hands of people, how can He truly be trusted?

Our Focus

1 Samuel 12:14,15—If you fear the LORD and serve and obey Him and do not rebel against His commands, and if both you and the king who reigns over you follow the LORD your God--good! But if you do not obey the LORD, and if you rebel against His commands, His hand will be against you, as it was against your fathers.

Romans 13:2—Consequently, he who rebels against the authority is rebelling against what God has instituted, and those who do so will bring judgment on themselves.

I Keep Asking

While occasionally there is the unique rebel born kicking and screaming who stays that way, most come to the place of resistance through hurt and pain. Many have a deep need to be valued, heard and unconditionally loved. We must also understand that there are times when it is appropriate to rebel. When leadership goes against God's clear directive standing against those misguided authorities is appropriate. Rebels often cause people to think. They may inspire needed action. Principled rebels founded many nations. But we are not examining these heroes.

Instead we look at those whose attitudes and actions cause dissension in the body of Christ and breed mutiny against God's truth. Rebellion as with most obstacles, is founded on pride. The rebel camps on the platform of personal rights and refuses to bend before God or man. Consequently, a rebel cannot grow very intimate with God for ultimately the man or woman who resists yielding to anyone in authority resists yielding to the Lord. In Exodus 23:20, God said to the Israelites:

See, I am sending an angel ahead of you to guard you along the way and to bring you to the place I have prepared. Pay attention to him and listen to what he says. Do not rebel against him; he will not forgive your rebellion, since my Name is in him.

Solomon wrote, **"Pride only breeds quarrels, but wisdom is found in those who take advice"** (Pro.13:10). I can share from personal experience that working with rebels not only is spiritually draining, but it also seems to keep God from blessing a body of believers that should be growing. There is an unhealthy tension present. Fellowship is degraded. Instead of believers focusing their attention on God they are left struggling with those intent on making a ruckus.

Are you a rebel? May I ask you to answer this question truthfully? Are you growing in your walk with God, at peace with His leading in your life, at rest with those around you? Or, do you constantly feel like you are engaging others in battle, restless, ill at ease with yourself and God? If the latter is true, may I suggest it is time to lay down your arms, ask God to forgive you for questioning Him, make peace with those with whom you struggle and rest. With humility comes the quiet you so desperately want. You have fought long to protect yourself. Now it is time to let God fight for you, to trust that He does know what is best. He will exalt you and you will grow if you will cease your resistance.

Will those you have regularly questioned hurt you? Probably—sin will not go away until Jesus comes. Will your observations be right? Most likely—but right at the expense of growth is a sorry proposition. Stop focusing on the deficiencies of those around you. Cease doubting God. Let Him lead and let Him work through His servants. We need you to be on the team—you matter!

Inspiration

 David--I said "No." The little boy looked up at his mother, back to the shelf, back to mother, back to the shelf and went for it. 3 (sic) year-old hands darted out. Grabbed hold of the item. And ran . . . When God says "No" it doesn't mean "maybe." When He calls, it doesn't mean "think about it, if you have a moment." Which is a hard message for you and I who are so used to living as the consumer-king, getting what we want, pampering our own desires and hitting the remote control if what we see or hear doesn't immediately suit our whim.—Pastor Ken Gehrels

Rebellion is the very spirit of Satan's attitude (Eph. 2:2), and if we permit it to dominate us it will infect and taint our attitude toward all authority, including God and His Word.—Dr. Dale A. Robbins

SARCASM

> ## Our Focus
> Ephesians 4:29—Do not let any unwholesome talk come out of your mouths, but only what is helpful for building others up according to their needs, that it may benefit those who listen.

Growing up, I was the butt of "short-people" jokes. Remember the song that came out in the '80's making fun of short people—"short people got no reason to live"? Unfortunately, I learned early on that an effective defense against cutting remarks was the use of sarcasm. A witty putdown is a form of art. It feels good to sting the stinger. But does it really?

James wrote:

Likewise the tongue is a small part of the body, but it makes great boasts. Consider what a great forest is set on fire by a small spark. The tongue also is a fire, a world of evil among the parts of the body. It corrupts the whole person, sets the whole course of his life on fire, and is itself set on fire by hell (James 3:5,6).

Imagine the next time you utter a sarcastic remark that your words set the person to whom you spoke on fire. Knowing how much a burn hurts and scars, is that what you really want to do to someone else? Sarcasm reveals that my strength is not in the Lord but rather in my tongue. Just as I can be wounded by another's remarks, so can I lacerate by being sarcastic. Yet, how can I gain intimacy with the Lord if I am incinerating His children?

Sarcasm is an indicator of insecurity. Those who are strong in the Lord do not use words to belittle those around them. It truly is amazing how much our speech reveals our walk with God.

The mark of a believer is not to wound others when badgered but to edify them. The Bible nowhere commends us for verbally stabbing those who provoke with their words or behavior. Instead God challenges us to speak words that build others up. The next time you feel a witty putdown-- stuff it. Be like Jesus who bore the insults of the religious elite and chose to love them.

He was oppressed and treated harshly, yet He never said a word. He was led as a lamb to the slaughter. And as a sheep is silent before the shearers, He did not open His mouth (Isa.53:7— NLT).

Inspiration

Cynicism is cancer of the spirit. The bad cells of sarcasm attack the good cells of hope and, if undiagnosed, will eventually destroy them.—Fred Smith

Sarcasm is the weapon of a weak, spiteful nature, its literal meaning is to tear the flesh from the bone.— Oswald Chambers in *The Pilgrim's Song Book*

A loose tongue renders all religion absolutely <u>worthless</u>!— David Wilkerson

TEMPTATION

> ## Our Focus
>
> Matthew 6:13; 26:41—And lead us not into temptation, but deliver us from the evil one . . . Watch and pray so that you will not fall into temptation. The spirit is willing, but the body is weak.

Upstairs I have a resident called Mind. I've learned over time that he frequently receives an unwelcome entity. This intruder can be obnoxious, devious and overbearing while at other times smooth and spellbinding. His name is Temptation. His goal is to captivate Mind so he can have his own way. And he'd like to do the same to your Mind.

Temptation is not sin—even Jesus was tempted (Mat.4:1). Hebrews 4:15 says, **This High Priest of ours understands our weaknesses, for He faced all of the same temptations we do, yet He did not sin** (NLT). The difference between Jesus and us is that He <u>always</u> said "No" to sin. He gave no lodging to evil desires. *Abnegation* is not easy. But our minds cannot be overcome by temptation unless we give in. The Bible encourages us with this truth:

But remember that the temptations that come into your life are no different from what others experience. And God is faithful. He will keep the temptation from becoming so strong that you can't stand up against it. When you are tempted, He will show you a way out so that you will not give in to it (1 Co.10:13 NLT).

Temptation becomes an obstacle to our relationship with God when we let it seize us and fail to look for a way out. Scantily clad females tempt me. Anyplace I go that attracts women dressed provocatively I'm setting myself up for trouble. The way to defeat temptation is to avoid lingering around places that will pull my mind in the wrong direction.

There is always a way to escape temptation. Honestly, our problem is like Robert Orbin says, "Most people want to be delivered from temptation but would like to keep in touch."

Temptations like lust remain personal. While God has the ability to read our thoughts, those around us may have no idea we are under temptation. For this reason, we need to flee whatever entices us to do wrong. Joseph is my Bible hero when it comes to resisting temptation. When his boss' s wife said day after day, "Come to bed with me!" (Gen.39), he refused. When she noticed she was alone with him in the house and she put her hands on his cloak and again invited him to have sex with her, he ran! Are we willing to run!

What evil desires lurk in the shadows of your mind? What temptations own you? Don't let the mind's playground turn into a spiritual graveyard.

Inspiration

G.H. Charnley, in *The Skylark's Bargain*, tells the story of a young skylark who discovered one day a man who would give him worms for a feather. He struck a bargain--one feather for two worms. The next day the lark was flying high in the sky with his father when the older bird said, "You know, son, we skylarks should be the happiest of all birds. See our brave wings! They lift us high in the air, nearer and nearer to God." But the young bird did not hear him. All he saw was an old man with worms. Down he flew, plucked two feathers from his wings and had a feast. For days this continued until autumn arrived and it was time to fly south. But the young skylark could not fly with his family. He had exchanged the power of his young wings for worms. That is our constant temptation in life--to exchange wings for worms.

Survey respondents noted temptations were more potent when they had neglected their time with God (81 percent) and when they were physically tired (57 percent). Resisting temptation was accomplished by prayer (84 percent), avoiding compromising situations (76 percent), Bible study (66 percent), and being accountable to someone (52 percent).—*Discipleship Journal*, 11-12/1992.

VACILLATION

Julius Caesar led his army across a short river of north central Italy in 49 B.C. to launch a civil war. The name of the river was Rubicon a name now synonymous with irrevocable commitment. When Caesar and his men crossed the river, there was no turning back. They were determined to fight to death if that's what it took.

Our Focus

Ruth 1:16—But Ruth replied, "Don't urge me to leave you or to turn back from you. Where you go I will go, and where you stay I will stay. Your people will be my people and your God my God."

A Jewish woman named Naomi lost her husband and her sons while living in the land of Moab. When she heard that the famine besieging Judah had ended she decided to return home. Her two daughters-in-law, Orpah and Ruth, followed but she tearfully told them to go back to their own land, kissed them and tried sending them away. Finally Orpah relented and bade her goodbye, and went her way. Ruth however, refused to go back! She uttered the gutsy words written in the verse above and Naomi gave up trying to dissuade her. The two of them pressed on, crossed the Arnon River and followed the road that would lead them to Naomi's hometown--Bethlehem.

God rewarded the Moabite maiden with a wonderful husband Boaz. Ruth became the great-grandmother of King David, from whose lineage Jesus would one day be born. She was blessed for being faithful and persevering. You can read her marvelous story in the Old Testament book of Ruth.

Are you still wandering in Vacillation Valley? Why! What will it take for you to get serious about following God? When will you cross the river? When will your neck not tire from turning left and right at the expense of FORWARD MARCH! Jesus bought you with His life and He means for you to get serious serving Him. There is no glory in wavering. There is no fruit in half-hearted limbs.

At the core of vacillation is liquid fear—unstable and nauseating! Get rid of it! Trust God. Set your eyes on Jesus. Don't take the winding way back when faced with challenge and difficulty. That way swerves with every shift in the wind. Be like Rubicon Ruth and cross the river! You won't regret it! Now get going before you miss the boat.

Inspiration

Much of life is a moral and spiritual journey, and it makes no sense to send young people forth on such a journey having offered them only some timid, vacillating opinions about proper conduct. We must give your children better equipment than that. We must offer them unequivocal, reliable standards of right and wrong, noble and base, just and unjust. We must treat life as a moral endeavor.—William Bennett

Vacillation in a crisis is the sign of an unabandoned nature. An abandoned nature cannot vacillate because there is nothing to weigh; it is completely abandoned to God.—Oswald Chambers in *Not Knowing Where*

QUITTING

Our Focus

2 Corinthians 13:5,6—Examine yourselves to see if your faith is really genuine. Test yourselves. If you cannot tell that Jesus Christ is in you, it means you have failed the test. (NLT)

If forty is an age for contemplation than here is a provocative observation. Failure ending in disappointment with God often begins on a trail of good intentions.

➤ A businessman started a homeless shelter only to see it collapse after five hard years. Today he ignores the Heavenly Father Who was not there for him.

➤ A journalist won't read her Bible or be seen in any gathering of Christians because her best scripture-quoting friend gossiped and she has been shamed. How could a loving God permit such back-stabbing!

➤ A grandfather is bitter. His eyes hang below his mouth with the unmistakable look of defeat. Christian businessmen defrauded him--more interested in his money than his heart. God let him down. His pride won't let him look back up.

Could quitting be the result of falling in love with the wrong god? If my ministry surpasses my relationship to Jesus, what distinguishes it from idolatry? If my reputation matters more than my Savior, what is my love really made of? If my well-being and motivation are staked to the quality of life I enjoy, how do I view God when a tornado strikes? If family comes first, where do I turn if my teenager rebels?

My motivation when I wake up must be to love Jesus. Anything short of that propels me to ruin. My victory when I turn out the lights must be Christ or my perspective is already jaded. Don't let your mind assume what your heart insists is best. God may graciously crush your dreams to enable you to see Him. The heart can be deceitful.

My goal was to be a missionary. I spent my life preparing to go. God said "No." to my plans. While I thought I was preparing to move overseas during my time in Seminary, He was preparing me to become a pastor in Oregon. He used the fangs of a slow moving, inoperable and deadly brain-stem tumor in my oldest son to rearrange our lives. He mercifully stripped me of what was good so that I could understand what was best. The potential loss of my three year-old Bryan in 1991, helped me see with new eyes God's loving Son.

Could I serve Jesus if Bryan died? What strength would I draw upon after hearing his doctor describe his tumor as "a ticking time bomb"? It would have been easy to quit and cry foul. I so vividly remember sobbing in the parking lot of our church in San Diego. The painful thought of losing Bryan was overwhelming. But we didn't quit. God is gracious and He gave us the strength to go on. The rest of the story is pretty amazing, but I'll save it for later!

What matters most is not family or career, health or prestige, work or recreation, but soul-sincere, heart-embracing, integrity-laced, truth-clutching, gut-inspiring, sin-quenched, chill-producing, worship-inducing, love for God. Failure is taking our eyes off Jesus. Quitting is refusing to see Him. Don't do it! You won't regret it!

Inspiration

It is not lack of spiritual experience that leads to failure, but lack of laboring to keep the ideal right.—Oswald Chambers in *My Utmost For His Highest*

Let spiritual progress be a driving passion in your life. How is this evidenced? By not quitting!—Pastor John A. Holt

Faithfulness has to do with what you do when *everything else around you screams for you to quit.*—Pastor Don Horban

I Keep Asking

PART III:
HOW TO KNOW WE ARE
GROWING

A spiritual marker identifies a time of transition, decision, or direction when I clearly know that God has guided me.— Henry T. Blackaby & Claude V. King in *Experiencing God*

God loves us the way we are, but he loves us too much to leave us that way.--Leighton Ford

How important it is that we remember that our God is far greater than our obstacles. Charles Hadden Spurgeon said, "The Lord's mercy often rides to the door of our heart upon the black horse of affliction." Suffering either finishes us or remodels us to be more like Jesus. Paul wrote the Corinthians, **"Therefore, since through God's mercy we have this ministry, we do not lose heart"** (2 Co.4:1). This verse helped me cope when my son's life hung in balance. I realized that ministry was not validated by my spiritual gifts or by an organization's approval, or by how healthy my family was. It is not just ministry that requires God's mercy, but life itself! His mercy brings us through trials! His mercy allows us to serve Him and to have sweet communion with Him. If we will look closely in the mirror, we will find mercy is a wonderful reflection—we see less of ourselves and more of Him.

I would rather run along a trail then around a track. It's much harder for me to remain motivated making the same circle repetitively. Before I run in the woods or along a path though, I like to get on my mountain bike and determine where my mile markers are. The way I evaluate my fitness is by scanning the time that has elapsed between markers. Just as I find it helpful to evaluate my physical condition, so do I need markers to help me see how I'm doing in my relationship with God. He has a faithful way of taking me over mountains and through the valleys. Staying in the same place may be comfortable but it does not facilitate growth.

High in the Alps is a monument raised in honor of a faithful guide who perished while ascending a peak to rescue a stranded tourist. Inscribed on that memorial stone are these words: HE DIED CLIMBING. A maturing, growing Christian should have the same kind of attitude, right up to the end of life.

Our American society, seems to be in a giant rush to retire. Yet the paradox is that those who have retired are rarely appreciated and, in fact, are often considered a nuisance. In Asia young people are still taught to show respect, to be humble and polite in the presence of those who have walked the earth for a long time. I am told it is the same in most parts of Africa, the Middle East and South America. When any society values speed over wisdom look for a lot of wrecked lives both old and young. Our responsibility as Christians is to value the journey of walking after God and to understand how we are progressing. The longer we travel the more godly we should become, the more wisdom we should amass. And friends, there is no such thing as retirement for God's children! Show me in the Bible where people retired, ceased serving God to kick back and enjoy the last summers of life and what we will find is people who were in sin, who left a legacy of shame and tragedy.

To know God, means to walk after Him until no more steps can be taken! Those who understand this leave a legacy that echoes glory to God in the highest mountains and the deepest ravines. Few things are more thrilling than spending time with withered saints whose skin may be sallow but whose heartsongs crackle with the roaring love for God that warms any blessed to be near. I want their love! I want their diligence! They wouldn't think of taking a vacation from God. They laugh at the notion of forsaking the climb! Their lives bear the fruit of faithfulness. Their prayers are that we would be faithful!

Would you like to be like the old heroes of the faith? Do you wonder if you are still spiritually maturing? Do you see God's mercy at work in your life? If someone asked you if you were growing in Christ how would you answer him? I believe there are distinct markers we can identify on our journey to know God. In this book we will examine twenty of these markers. In our next book, *I Pray Also* there are twenty more markers. These markers are arranged alphabetically and are useful for determining if we are headed in the right direction—towards our Father in heaven.

I KEEP ASKING ARE YOU . . . ?
ADAPTABLE

For six nights my kids slept in a tent I set up for them in our backyard. I figured they would last one night. But no—they loved the adventure and asked each evening to sleep outside. Even Dusty, our middle-aged lab retriever seemed more than happy to join them.

A Singaporean couple gave us a car they were not using. For some mechanical reason beyond my understanding, it would not go in reverse. So if I drove the Mitsubishi I had to make sure not to park in such a way that I would be stuck. This often called for some pretty creative driving!

Our Focus

1 Timothy 6:6-8—But godliness with contentment is great gain. For we brought nothing into the world, and we can take nothing out of it. But if we have food and clothing, we will be content with that.

2 Corinthians 11:27—I have labored and toiled and have often gone without sleep; I have known hunger and thirst and have often gone without food; I have been cold and naked.

I wonder if adaptability becomes more difficult with age. We grow accustomed to living each day in a predictable fashion. Over time how can we help not venerating custom and procedure, convenience and control at the expense of being flexible?

If I lost my home and had to live in a tent could I do it? Would I pull my stiff bones off the hard ground and see fit to praise God? Would I find joy in Jesus if it meant adapting to circumstances not of my own choosing? I hope so.

The test of loving God is not just how well I sing to Him when life is a slice of pie but how well I follow Him when hell's missiles seem to fall where I walk. I love God—more so with each passing day. I hope that in the great journey of serving Him what matters is not godliness based on convenience but rather godliness with contentment. I hope I don't have to have my way to think life is good. What I want is what God wants.

I don't suppose the angels spend time in heaven glorying in their pristine environment. I imagine their focus and praise is devoted to the epitome of awesomeness—Almighty God. **Marker #1 is our ability to adapt.** If our focus is on God we can get through anything. If our eyes are not on Jesus—look out!

Inspiration

Adaptability is the power to make a suitable environment for oneself out of any set of circumstances.—Oswald Chambers in *Not Knowing Where*

Understanding what God is about to do where I am is more important than telling God what I want to do for Him.—Henry T. Blackaby & Claude V. King in *Experiencing God*

Consideration
Marker #1: Adaptability
Personal Inventory
I know I am growing in my relationship with God because I am adaptable in:

_____

_____

_____

_____

_____

ASKING

Our Focus

2 Timothy 1:3—I thank God, whom I serve, as my fore-fathers did, with a clear conscience, as night and day I con-stantly remember you in my prayers.

My mother died of cancer when I was nine. She composed a special prayer for me that she would often take to God on my behalf. I didn't know about this prayer until a special friend, Georgia Drake, gave it to me after I was married and had my own children. Today, I still get tears in my eyes as I read the words my mom wrote. They are a reminder to me of how precious it is to love your children and to pray for them. They are a testimony to the power of prayer. They are words that have helped keep me safe and centered on the narrow path that leads home.

Build Me A Son
by Elizabeth Helen York

Build me a son, Heavenly Father, who loves You more than himself or others.
Build me a son who receives his orders for the day from You before he meets a man.
Build me a son who has in him the attributes You possess:

♦ Love: that sent Christ to die for us.
♦ Gentleness: that leads us like a shepherd;
♦ Joy: that fills our hearts to overflowing;
♦ Long-suffering: that never tires under stress;
♦ Goodness: that showers others with blessing upon blessing;

- Faith: that he may always know Your perfect will for him;
- Meekness: that he may see himself as Your humble servant;
- Honesty: that he may be known as a man of truth;
- Chastity: that his heart may be pure toward women and men;
- Giving: that spirit that gives to others continually;
- Comfort: that he may know how to weep with the sorrowful;
- Wisdom: that makes him not worldly wise, but a godly man;
- Submissive: that he will possess a servant's spirit toward You and others.

Build me a son who when he is old enough, will let You, his Heavenly Father, choose a helpmate for him that will draw him closer to You through the years, and will always be a godly and submissive wife.

I would rather hang my coat with one genuine intercessor and strong prayer warrior than a thousand who consider prayer a precursor to eating and a transition to meeting. And after reading Bruce Wilkinson's marvelous short book entitled *The Prayer of Jabez,* I would hate to stand before God someday and find out I missed blessings He intended to give me because I failed to ask!

Tucked in the midst of nine chapters of genealogies in the book of 1 Chronicles are two profound verses:

Jabez was more honorable than his brothers. His mother had named him Jabez, saying, 'I gave birth to him in pain.' Jabez cried out to the God of Israel, 'Oh, that you would bless me and

enlarge my territory! Let your hand be with me, and keep me from harm so that I will be free from pain.' And God granted his request" (1 Chr.4:9-10).

Why did God answer the request of Jabez? I believe he was asking with a good heart and what he asked pleased God. What better blessing can we have than God's blessing?

Have you ever noticed how free children feel to ask their parents for things? Granted what they ask for may not be wise, but what is refreshing is their honest approach. Because I love my children I take joy in fulfilling their requests if I am able and I believe it to be in their best interest. Don't be afraid to come to your Heavenly Father with your needs. He says He cares so present your concerns. **Marker #2 is our willingness to seek God's help.** Jesus taught us, **"Ask and it will be given to you; seek and you will find; knock and the door will be opened to you"** (Mat.7:7). As we grow, one of the things we notice is that we become wiser and more selective about what we ask from God.

Inspiration

When you pray, things remain the same, but you begin to be different.—Oswald Chambers in *If You Will Ask*

Prayer pulls the rope down below and the great bell rings above in the ears of God. Some scarcely stir the bell, for they pray so languidly; others give only an occasional jerk at the rope. But he who communicates with heaven is the man who grasps the rope boldly and pulls continuously with all his might.—C.H. Spurgeon

Give me one hundred preachers who fear nothing but sin and desire nothing but God, and I care not a straw whether they be clergymen or laymen; such alone will shake the gates of hell and set up the kingdom of heaven on earth. God does nothing but in answer to prayer.—John Wesley

Consideration
Marker #2: Asking
Personal Inventory

I know I am growing in my relationship with
God because I am asking Him to:

_____

_____

_____

_____

Have you ever considered keeping a log of prayer requests
with the date and manner in which God answered?

ATTENTIVE

Our Focus

2 Timothy 2:15—Do your best to present yourself to God as one approved, a workman who does not need to be ashamed and who correctly handles the word of truth.

It's really embarrassing when someone asks a question and I can't answer it because I was daydreaming. Ever have that happen to you in school? The secret to effective communication is paying attention, truly listening. The beauty of being attentive, really attentive, is that we have a firmer grasp of the big picture and of the details.

Remember when I shared how I botched my floor initially by not following the directions and utilizing the correct tools. Before I installed my floor I purchased an unassembled home entertainment center knowing my limited construction skills would be challenged. I'm just not very skilled when it comes to building things. I'd be a natural guest for Home Improvement comedies! But so long as I followed the excellent by-the-numbers directions and had help from my good friend Dan, I figured I'd be fine. I worked late into the night and was quite pleased with the emerging work of art.

Dan stopped by the next morning and immediately pointed out that I'd put a key piece in backwards. I had to disassemble the wood to fix the error. Later when we tried to put the doors on I found that I'd omitted a minor step early in the directions that again disrupted the project. What should have been a half-day project turned into a three-day exercise in frustration. Thank God for friends that know how to build!

Spiritual Markers

The Apostle Paul encouraged his apprentice Timothy, to do his best in serving God. He used the word picture of a workman polished in his skills. His words serve as a reminder that when we serve God we ought to pay attention to what we are doing. Just as a piece of furniture can be incorrectly assembled and ultimately dysfunctional, so when we improperly use God's word we can damage others and ourselves. It takes no skill to be careless. It takes hard work and discernment to be accurate.

Kevin Adams served as the Chairman of our Leadership Council in Horizon Community Church, the first church I pastored. Kevin once shared with our men about the time he served on a church-building project. He was pounding down a twisted nail into a board on the roof when one of the leaders asked him if he would do such a thing on his own roof. As Kevin realized that he was truly working for the Lord it changed his whole approach to projects.

Marker #3 is our ability to listen and be attentive. Spiritual builders must have great attention to detail. We dare not misrepresent God and His word. We cannot be shoddy in the way we live our lives. Shame comes from lack of preparation and poor execution. Joy comes from knowing we followed God's instruction carefully so that He is glorified.

Attention to detail may seem like a hassle but believe me, it sure proves worthwhile in the end. **"And whatever you do, whether in word or deed, do it all in the name of the Lord Jesus, giving thanks to God the Father through Him"** (Col.3:17).

Inspiration

All things hinge upon your hearty renunciation of everything which you are aware does not lead to God.—Brother Lawrence in *Practicing His Presence*

Attention is never possible without conscious effort; . . . We all have certain native interests in which we are absorbed, but attention is always an effort of will. We are held responsible by God for the culture of attention.—Oswald Chambers in *The Moral Foundations of Life*

Consideration

Marker #3: Attentive
Personal Inventory
I know I am growing in my relationship with God because I am attentive in:

_____

_____

_____

_____

_____

BALANCED

> ## Our Focus
>
> Psalm 54:4—Surely God is my help; the Lord is the One Who sustains me.
>
> 73:26—My flesh and my heart may fail, but God is the strength of my heart and my portion forever.

Kathleen and I ascended as the elevator began to shake noisily. The two women beside us discussed when the old box was going to fall, evidently used to its rattle. But as we walked into the office there on the eighth floor we noticed the building swaying. It was an eerie feeling. Less than 150 miles away, Olympia and Seattle were riding a major earthquake. Yet we were safe. The receptionist informed us that the building was constructed to bend a foot or more during quakes so as not to collapse. Thank God for good engineering.

Tremors test the integrity of our structure. They also reveal our convictions and habits. Adversity tests how we are doing in our quest to know God. If we are secure in our relationship with Him we maintain spiritual equilibrium in the day-to-day living as well as in the midst of dirt-moving trials. We recognize that our strength comes in the Lord. He is the One Who sustains us. Redemption has permanently countered the effect of sin and afforded us hope while on an evil earth.

Are you spiritually balanced? **Our 4th marker along the journey is balance.** Do you emerge through conflict, pain and trauma with your faith intact? Do those around you see stability in your perspective and quiet confidence in your character? Do you live your life with a quiet consistency that reveals the Holy Spirit's leadership? Are you able to set aside what is less important to focus on what is most vital? Do you eat right, get enough rest and exercise regularly so that your temple is maintained properly? If not, get out of the sinkhole caused by building on sand and start building on the Rock!

Inspiration

Absorption in practical work is one of the greatest hindrances to discerning the call of God. Unless active work is balanced by a deep, isolated solitude with God, knowledge of God does not grow and the worker becomes exhausted and spent. Our Lord said that the only men He can use in His enterprises are those in whom He has done everything (see Luke 14:26-27, 33); otherwise we serve our own ends all the time.—Oswald Chambers in *Not Knowing Where*

Holiness means a perfect balance between our disposition and the laws of God.—Oswald Chambers in **Studies in the Sermon on the Mount**

Consideration

Marker #4: Balanced
Personal Inventory

Here's a simple test to evaluate if you are balanced in your Christian life:

	Yes	No
1. I exercise regularly	____	____
2. I get good sufficient sleep	____	____
3. I eat a healthy diet	____	____
4. I drink plenty of water	____	____
5. I have a clean conscience	____	____
6. I don't let conflict go unresolved	____	____
7. I set aside regular time to meet with God	____	____
8. I am able to prioritize my work load	____	____
9. I run to God first when I am in trouble	____	____
10. I give my burdens to the Lord to carry	____	____

CEDARS

We signed up for a hike with a ranger, who told us a remarkable thing: when a tree's life is threatened, stressed by the elements of fire, drought, or other calamity, it twists beneath its bark to reinforce and make itself stronger. On the surface, this new inner strength may not be visible, for the bark often continues to give the same vertical appearance. Only when the exterior is stripped away, or when the tree is felled are its inner struggles revealed.—Marilyn J. Abraham in *First We Quit Our Jobs*

Oswald Chambers in his book *Workmen of God*, noted that the cedars of Lebanon have such extraordinary power of life that instead of nourishing parasites they kill them. Are you so strong in your relationship with God that you are able to kill temptation, to keep sin from taking root in your life?

I Keep Asking

I can tell myself I'm a pretty good guy and try to live in my own power but let's face it—the end result reeks. I was so aware of this thought one day that I wrote a song entitled "Lord I'm In the Battle." Here are the words to the song*:

LORD, I'M IN THE BATTLE

Lord, I'm in the battle in a fight against the flames
All around confusion, too many voices airing blame,
so many questions . . .
Before I'm hurt and wounded may You find me on my knees
believing in Your promises, in Your light where I can see.

Never let me march to war unless Your banner leads the way.
The gates of hell cannot prevail against the power of
Your name.
Lord I choose to follow only help me to obey!
May I be Your humble servant and live for You today.

Lord, I'm in the battle and I must admit the shame
for the times You found me sleeping
when I should have been awake.
How could I deny You when You gave Your life for me?
O Everlasting Savior just let me worship at Your feet.

Lord, I'm in the battle and I know it's not a game,
Hearts around me broken in the shadow of the graves,
so many questions.
As the drums are beating and the walls are falling down
let the trumpets sound for Jesus, the Savior of the world.*

My mind lusts, my eyes covet, my nature is inherently selfish. In short, there is a war going on. Every person on this planet is engaged daily in war--Flesh against Spirit. Whenever I choose the side of Flesh, life invariably gets miserable and hell has a shopping spree. Whenever I yield to

*©1999 Dan York CHOICES CD ARR.

God's Spirit, life becomes joyful and all heaven breaks loose. This is not an oversimplification of a classic struggle, just the confessions of a battle veteran.

Our Focus

Galatians 5:16,17--So I say, live {walk} by the Spirit, and you will not gratify the desires of the sinful nature. For the sinful nature desires what is contrary to the Spirit, and the Spirit what is contrary to the sinful nature. They are in conflict with each other so that you do not do what you want.

Hebrews 12:4—In your struggle against sin, you have not yet resisted to the point of shedding your blood.

Climbing the staircase to LTC Mark Armstrong's office one cannot help but notice the words painted between steps: Loyalty, Duty, Respect, Selfless service, Honor, Integrity and Personal courage. These are seven key values the Army seeks to instill in all its soldiers. They are values that Mark takes seriously as the Battalion Commander of the 1st Battalion of the 46th Infantry.

Young men from around the nation assemble at Fort Knox, Kentucky. They enter companies a motley meld of self-centered individuals. Those who graduate Basic Training nine weeks later emerge as team-oriented soldiers, radically transformed before the eyes of their incredulous parents and friends.

Mark, ascertains first-hand why values are important. Each day he watches drill instructors work with men who often come from broken families. He sees self-centered rookies; grown children unaccustomed to persevering through adversity; privates whose idea of loyalty is looking out for #1; individuals who can barely define integrity or exemplify honor. If these men refused the challenge of embracing values or were part of an organization without a moral compass, they would help create a treacherous society bent on feeding untamed lusts. It is no wonder this seasoned officer's eyes fill with tears. He can share countless stories of changed lives. He cherishes imparting truth to a generation fed on materialism, relativism and intolerance for adversity. He understands why it is necessary for soldiers to obediently low crawl in mud below barbed wire while life-ending tracers whiz overhead. Mark knows what happens at the other end. (Mark is pictured on page 47, 1st person on the left).

Values are not priceless because they come easy. We do not become godly by being lazy or righteous by pleasing our flesh. If we are serious about loving God, He will seriously work to test our mettle, to break what is corrupted to create what is incorruptible. Jesus taught that we must be robed in self-denial and refuse to leave the narrow path no matter how easy the broad road looks. Did Jesus struggle? Ask the centurion who watched Him die. Was His sacrifice worth it? Ask the sinner who understands what it means to be pardoned and given eternal life.

Yes, Lord, I'm in the battle. I'm so thankful You're the Commander. With You in charge, sin will one day be vanquished! May we listen to You, embrace godly values, so we are able to withstand sin. **Marker #5 is our ability to resist sin**. Are you a cedar?

Inspiration

The harder the conflict, the more glorious the triumph. What we obtain too cheap, we esteem too lightly; 'tis dearness only that gives everything its value.—Thomas Paine

Consideration
Marker #5: Resistance
Personal Inventory

I know I am growing in my relationship with
God because I am saying "no" to:

_____

_____

_____

_____

CONFIDENT

> ### Our Focus
> Philippians 4:13—I can do everything through Him who gives me strength.

- ◆ It looked impossible. How could a little church of fifty build a sanctuary and lease the commercial space necessary for classrooms an office, bathrooms plus the large meeting room for worship?
- ◆ Jeff was exhausted. He'd poured out his heart before God into people but he felt like there was no strength to continue. How could he face the people tomorrow if he couldn't face himself today?
- ◆ Sally's children were running her into a place of despair. Their nonstop energy and knack for finding trouble left her feeling like the twenty-year old sweater hanging on the door. "Oh God! I can't raise these kids they're too much to handle!"

There's a saying we call a truism—"People who say can't--don't!" Are you feeling discouraged or defeated? Do you feel perhaps God asks too much of you? Are you afraid to really know Him? **Marker #6 is confidence that what matters in walking through life is that we can do all things through Christ Who gives us strength!**

In my life, the greatest tests to my confidence in God usually revolve around money. In leading **Encounter Ministries**, our nonprofit organization, my family is challenged every month to rely on the Lord to bring in enough finances for us to pay our bills and minister as He has called us. If I said it was easy to trust God, I'd be stretching the truth. It is not. But it sure is exciting! Every month our Father in heaven brings in exactly what we need through our ministry sponsors, unexpected gifts, or work with the Army

Reserves. I learned early on in life watching my parents that God faithfully provides. There has never been a time in my life when I have seen God fail to honor His promise to take care of us. I do believe Jesus was speaking to us when He said in Mat.6:25-27:

Therefore I tell you, do not worry about your life, what you will eat or drink; or about your body, what you will wear. Is not life more important than food, and the body more important than clothes? Look at the birds of the air; they do not sow or reap or store away in barns, and yet your heavenly Father feeds them. Are you not much more valuable than they? Who of you by worrying can add a single hour to his life?

We do not carry credit card debt. We do not manipulate people for assistance. We do not live in fear. My children are growing up and learning that God is awesome. He lovingly provides. If He calls us to minister, He provides the resources we need. If we share our concerns, He comforts and guides—not always in the way we expect but always for His glory. It is impossible to be confident and yet be immobilized by worry at the same time. We either believe God can or we don't!

Remember the children's story about the little engine that said, "I think I can, I think I can!" Praise God, I can say, "I know I can, I know I can!" Can you? In Christ nothing is impossible. The question we must ask is, are we "in Christ!" If so, we may walk with Him in confidence!

For I am convinced that neither death nor life, neither angels nor demons, neither the present nor the future, nor any powers, neither height nor depth, nor anything else in all creation, will be able to separate us from the love of God that is in Christ Jesus our Lord (Rom.8:38,39).

Inspiration

A saint is made by God, "He made me." Then do not tell God He is a bungling workman. We do that whenever we say, "I can't." To say "I can't" literally means we are too strong in ourselves to depend on God.—Oswald Chambers in *So Send I You*

When a saint puts his or her confidence in the election of God, no tribulation or affliction can ever touch that confidence.—Oswald Chambers in *Christian Disciplines*

Consideration

Marker #6: Confidence
Personal Inventory

Okay here's the deal. You want to gain confidence right?! Make a list of the five things you are most afraid of:

1._____
2._____
3._____
4._____
5._____

After prayer, careful consideration and perhaps the advice of someone you trust, pick one of the five fears above and tackle it. For example, if you are afraid of speaking in front of a group, ask your pastor or home group leader for an opportunity to publicly share your testimony. You get the idea. Trust the Lord to help you and build your confidence. Philippians 4:13 is yours for the application!

CONTENT WITH GODLY PERSPECTIVE

Drafting is such an amazing art. I find it fascinating how engineers depict buildings and objects through the skillful drawing of lines and shading areas. Did you know that perspective is defined in *The American Heritage Dictionary* as: "The technique of representing three-dimensional objects and depth relationships on a two-dimensional surface."

Could it be that spiritual perspective is the technique of representing an invisible God and the depth relationship of His attributes on the sin-flattened temporal plain of earth? When we love our enemies, we reveal God! When we demonstrate patience through adversity, our lives portray a supernatural dimension. The linear two-dimensioned relationship between humans becomes a three-dimensional triangle when God is involved.

Perspective also means *"A mental view or outlook."* True wisdom, therefore, is seeing things from God's perspective. When adversity comes, I want to know Jesus Who weathered hostility and was murdered. When temptation raises its stormy head I want to know Christ Who Himself suffered through temptation (Heb.2:18). When times are good, I want to know my Father and thank Him for what I have. When I am confused, I want to know the omniscient One. When I am weak I want to be close to the Almighty. When I am joyful, I want to worship my Savior! When I am honored, I want to glorify the Lord Who made me. Whether busy or inactive, tired or energetic, thoughtful or amused, balanced or dizzy, sick or healthy, fulfilled or discouraged, driven or grounded, criticized or praised, popular or opposed, filled or empty—I want to know God. How I view life is proportional to how well I know life's Creator.

I Keep Asking

I wonder if the "desert" experiences so many Christians endure is hastened by an unbalanced perspective of the Christian life. If we go to church expecting to be entertained; read our Bibles anticipating profound inspiration; enter prayer insisting God meet our conditions; and, if we are constantly looking for the latest spiritual trend; are we not in danger of trying to create the "mountain-top" euphoria that is not the stuff of daily living? What do you suppose Paul's thoughts were about the Ephesian believers when he wrote, **"I keep asking that the God of our Lord Jesus Christ, the glorious Father, may give you the Spirit of wisdom and revelation, so that you may know Him better"** (Eph.1:17).

We become content or fulfilled when we understand that God is concerned about the process as much as He is about the product. We need to be content during the journey. While fulfillment is about bringing closure to what was initiated, it also means "to measure up, to satisfy." How we define being fulfilled dictates what kind of life we will lead.

If I determine that I am my own captain, then my fulfillment is confined by what I can and cannot do. If I concede control of my life to others, then my fulfillment is defined by the will of those in power. If I believe that God is the One leading me, then my fulfillment rests in gripping firmly the rope of His will.

Henry Blackaby, wrote in his book *Experiencing God*, What is God's will for my life?—is *not* the right question. I think the right question is, What is God's will? Once I know God's will, then I can adjust my life to Him. In other words, what is it that God is purposing where I am. Once I know what God is doing, then I know what I need to do. The focus needs to be on *God*, not *my life*!

Are you feeling unfulfilled? Does your fruit basket seem empty? Don't despair! Don't drink from the pity pail your enemy loves to fill. Don't give up! God has never yet lost His will! He knows what is best for you and I and that best is always the accomplishment of His mission. Do not be afraid to stop what you are doing and wait upon the Lord for His guidance. Set aside preoccupation with what you don't know and discover what He is doing around you. Listen to His word and the leading of the Holy Spirit. If you will take your eyes off yourself and your circumstances and look for Him, He promises to lead you and never forsake you.

The secret to contentment is Jesus Christ, the Savior of the lost. We know it inside just like we know to floss! When will we have the strength to go after His will and trust His voice? Can you camp on the beach of desolation, eat from the can of hardship and sleep on the sand of uncertainty yet experience joy because your security is in your relationship to your heavenly Father? Can you live in the hamlet of prosperity with all its trappings, work a great job and yet measure fulfillment not by what you own or do but by obeying the voice of your King?

Our Focus

Philippians 3:8—What is more, I consider everything a loss compared to the surpassing greatness of knowing Christ Jesus my Lord, for whose sake I have lost all things. I consider them rubbish, that I may gain Christ.

4:12--I know what it is to be in need, and I know what it is to have plenty. I have learned the secret of being content in any and every situation, whether well fed or hungry, whether living in plenty or in want.

The test of our commitment to Christ and our ability to be useful to the Master is measured by our willingness to serve in the ordinary not the extraordinary. If we will be content to serve when life is devoid of fireworks, we will model the essence of what it means to live a Spirit-filled life. God is not looking for His children to exalt the ecstatic. He is looking for faithfulness. Perhaps the key to being faithful begins with being content. If you are more in love with Jesus today, and able to say with the Apostle Paul, "**I have learned the secret of being content in any and every situation**" then praise God! Your attitude is a sure indicator that you are growing through suffering and through prosperity! **Marker #7 is our ability to be content and to operate with a spiritual perspective.**

O God, stoke the passion to know You! Replace the selfish lens that see only me and cover them with Songlasses, those glorious lens that reveal You, the epitome of AWESOME!

Inspiration

We are not built for mountains and dawns and artistic affinities; they are for moments of inspiration, that is all. We are built for the valley, for the ordinary stuff of life, and this is where we have to prove our mettle.—Oswald Chambers in *My Utmost For His Highest*

Once when Diogenes was sunning himself, Alexander the Great visited him and said, "Ask any favor you wish from me." Diogenes responded, "Please move out of the sunlight." To which Alexander said, "If I could not be Alexander, I would be Diogenes." *—Bible Illustrator*

An ancient Persian legend tells of a wealthy man by the name of Al Haffed who owned a large farm. One evening a visitor related to him tales of fabulous amounts of diamonds that could be found in other parts of the world, and of the great riches they could bring him. The vision of all this wealth made him feel poor by comparison. So instead of caring for his own prosperous farm, he sold it and set out to find these treasures. But the search proved to be fruitless. Finally, penniless and in despair, he committed suicide by jumping into the sea. Meanwhile, the man who had purchased his farm noticed one day the glint of an unusual stone in a shallow stream on the property. He reached into the water, and to his amazement he pulled out a huge diamond. Later when working in his garden, he uncovered many more valuable gems. Poor Al Haffed had spent his life traveling to distant lands seeking jewels when on the farm he had left behind were all the precious stones his heart could have ever desired. *—Bible Illustrator*

Consideration

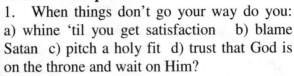

Marker #7: Contentment
Personal Inventory:
Take the Perspective Test:

1.   When things don't go your way do you: a) whine 'til you get satisfaction   b) blame Satan c) pitch a holy fit d) trust that God is on the throne and wait on Him?

Married People (Singles skip to Question 3)

2.   When your marriage is miserable do you: a) blame it on your spouse b) blame Satan   c) start divorce proceedings   d) take it to the Lord and work on problem-resolution?

3.   When your life seems aimless and God is nowhere to be found do you: a) continue to spend time in His Word and pray b) blame Satan   c) conclude God does not love you d) forget trying to be righteous.

4.   True or False. I'd rather read a best-selling Christian fiction series and talk about it with my Christian friends than read my Bible and discuss it with other believers.

5.   True or False. Most of the Christians I hang out with are better at whining than worship.

6.   True or False. My work, lifestyle, possessions, and status in life are more important than my walk with God.

7.   If my friends were asked what was #1 in my life they would answer: a) my pets b) my job c) my family d) my toys e) my relationship with God f) my spouse g) my reputation.

8.   True or False. I measure my spiritual condition by my state of happiness.

9.   True or False. I have not led anyone to Christ in over two years, I really don't have any nonbelieving friends and my complacency doesn't really bother me.

10. True or False. I don't tend to measure contentment by how well I am obeying God and His commands.

COURAGEOUS

Chinese fighter pilot Art Chen "took on three Japanese fighters and shot one down before running out of ammunition. He deliberately rammed the second Japanese plane, then bailed out. He landed close to the wreckage of his plane and salvaged one of the machine guns, which he carried eight miles back to the airfield. Presenting the heavy gun to his commanding officer, Chen allegedly asked, 'Sir, can I have another airplane for my machine gun?'"—Duane Schultz in *The Maverick War: Chennault and the Flying Tigers*

Faith Academy, Cainta Rizal Philippines

There will come a day, (you may be in one now), when you will be severely tested. Think it won't happen? As I am writing this, Martin and Gracie Burnham are in the hands of Muslim terrorists in the Philippines. Martin was my classmate at **Faith Academy** in high school. I remember he wanted to be a missionary pilot. Imagine my surprise when I read that he and his wife were kidnapped while working together on the island of Palawan.

Martin, by God's grace achieved his dream of piloting to serve God. He has three children who presently along with the rest of us, are unsure of what fate awaits their mom and dad. I have heard that he was wounded. But the best report to date came from a released hostage. This person reported that while the majority of the hostages prayed for God to work their release Martin just praised God. JUST PRAISED GOD! Now that's courage. You see, Martin has obviously learned to trust that his life is in God's hands and he need not be afraid whatever the danger.

What if your finances are suddenly ruined! Your family may feud and draw you into the conflict. Your body may be wracked by disease or a lingering malady that refuses to leave. You may be hurt by someone you deeply love. Your boss may question your competency. You may fail a test of critical importance. Your reputation may be slandered by one intent on causing you pain. You may go into a depression that is inexplicable. You may be involved in a head-on collision. Whatever your age or situation in life you can count on some form of trial or test coming your way. What kind of courage will you have?

Our Focus

Daniel 6:23—The king was overjoyed and gave orders to lift Daniel out of the (lion's) den. And when Daniel was lifted from the den, no wound was found on him, because he had trusted in his God.

Daniel, the Hebrew prophet and Jewish exile in Babylon, was thrown into the lion's den for refusing to quit praying to his God. Knowing that his king's edict could cost him his life, Daniel nevertheless bowed three times in prayer before a window that pointed in the direction of his homeland. He exercised courage! By setting aside his daily habit of prayer he would have been disloyal to God. Now granted, most of us will not be kidnapped like Martin, or tossed into a pit full of hungry lions like Daniel. Yet there may well come a day when our faith will be severely tested. **Our eighth marker is our ability to live courageously when in the midst of trials.**

In the last 100 years more Christians died for their faith than the sum total of all Christians martyred in every previous century. There are Chinese and Sudanese Christians right now, who are hiding because people who hate Christ want to destroy them. Courageously these heroes of the faith have endured the loss of family, jobs and safety because they bravely chose to become disciples of Jesus. They consider it a major blessing just to get their hands on the Word of God and to be able to read it. They covertly meet with other Christians for fellowship. They deserve our prayers and financial help. We should be on our knees thanking God for the freedom we have to worship Him.

May I invite you to take a 3x5 card and write in large bold letters the word "**COURAGE**". Beneath it write the reference Isa.41:10. This passage of promise reads, "**So do not fear, for I am with you; do not be dismayed, for I am your God. I will strengthen you and help you; I will uphold you with my righteous right hand.**" Now take that card and place it in your wallet or purse or position it in a place where you will constantly see it. When your test comes, and it will come, be a person of courage. Turn to Jesus Christ. Trust Him with your problems however great they are. He <u>will</u> see You through. He, the Lord of the Universe, personally loves you. So take courage!!!

168

Inspiration

We conquer in dying; we go forth victorious at the very time we are subdued . . .The blood of the martyrs is seed.—Quintus Septimus Florens Tertullian *(A great number of scholars believe that it was courageous example of Christian martyrs that led him to become a Christian near the end of the second century. Tertullian was arguably the great apologist of his time.)*

At the execution scene the soldiers began to secure him to the stake, but Polycarp stopped them: "Leave me as I am. For he who grants me to endure the fire will enable me also to remain on the pyre unmoved, without the security you desire from nails." He prayed and the fire was lit. The second-century chronicler of this martyrdom said it was "not as burning flesh but as bread baking or as gold and silver refined in a furnace." The martyrdom, he added, was remembered by "everyone"—"he is even spoken of by the heathen in every place."—Mark Galli in *Christianity Today*, May 19, 1997.

Consideration

Marker #8: Courageous
Personal Inventory
I know I am growing in my relationship with God because I have demonstrated courage by:

_____

_____

_____

_____

DECISIVE

"I'm so tired of that phone ringing," you mutter to yourself on your way down the stairs. "Do I answer it or do I let it ring!" A friend wants to know if you'll come over and look at patterns as she picks out new upholstery. At the same time your child screams from the highchair demanding more food. She needs to be disciplined but you're weary of the constant battles. The other kids still need lunches before they go to school and you still have to stop by the office sometime to get those crazy checks in the mail. All of this and your husband's upset because his tie is nowhere to be found.

Roger watches as Burt takes the cash. It's illegal but what the heck, they don't have to pay taxes this way. They just heard a message by their pastor last week on ethics. They've even discussed the fact that what they are doing is wrong but neither wants to take the first step to correcting the problem.

Sherry sobs away the night. Her husband is a sluggard. He won't help around the house and their marriage has lost all its former flavor. She knows she needs to say something to him but she is afraid. So she silently accumulates resentment and feels increasingly alienated from him.

Our Focus

1 Chronicles 14:13,14—Once more the Philistines raided the valley; so David inquired of God again, and God answered him, "Do not go straight up, but circle around them and attack them in front of the balsam trees."

Life is filled with decisions. Whether we're keeping the family straight, juggling ethical issues or combating interpersonal struggles, there is no end to the need to make decisions. King David is a great Biblical character to study when it comes to the arena of being decisive. When David was faced with a predicament he prayed. He made difficult decisions and then acted upon them. We won't get to know God very well if we allow our circumstances to control us.

We have to be decisive if we are ever going to handle problems and feed ourselves with spiritually nourishing food. We often hear we must escape the hustle and whir of activities to get time with the Lord. That is not necessarily true. Often, we need to bring God into the middle of our rush hour traffic and commune with Him. God doesn't require a rock and some quiet stream to sanction fellowship with us! He wants us to choose each moment that we can to come before Him. It's our choice.

What decision does God want you to make? If He has revealed what is wrong, don't be afraid to do what is right. He'll give you the strength to be holy and the wisdom to do the right thing. **Marker #9 is our ability to be decisive, to make the hard calls that will enable us to grow!**

Inspiration

A leader is a man who can burn his bridges behind him. Circumstances will not frustrate him, nor difficulties deter. Because his aim is single and his motive pure, his decisions are not complex and he does not vacillate.—J. Oswald Sanders in *A Spiritual Clinic*

Consideration

Marker #9: Decisive
Personal Inventory
I know I am growing in my relationship with God because I am decisively:_____

_____

_____

_____

_____

DILIGENT

The Kahiltna glacier feeds the broad Kahiltna River that in turn is joined by the clear running water of Peter's Creek. Where the fast moving milky river and the rippling creek meet is a place where thousands of King and Silver Salmon leave their river highway from the Pacific Ocean to return home and spawn. On the northwest side of the watery marriage, high above in a birch tree, is an eagle' nest. Eaglet's cries pierce the valley as they screech for food.

Atop nearby trees majestic bald eagles survey the land and water. With a graceful swoop, the mother drops below to sink her talons in an unsuspecting salmon. With powerful flaps, she ascends to her nest and attends her brood. It is a grandiose site in the great frontier of Alaska. One cannot help but be impressed by the diligence devoted eagles give in raising their young. Seagulls whose flight patterns run too close to the nest risk attack. No intruder goes unnoticed by the awe-inspiring Haliaeetus leucocephalus.

Our Focus

1 Timothy 4: 14-16—Do not neglect your gift, which was given you through a prophetic message when the body of elders laid their hands on you. Be diligent in these matters; give yourself wholly to them, so that everyone may see your progress. Watch your life and doctrine closely. Persevere in them, because if you do, you will save both yourself and your hearers.

The dictionary defines diligence as "painstaking effort". It costs something to be diligent. How closely do you watch your life and what you believe? Just as eagles persevere in feeding and caring for themselves and their young, so we ought to be steadfast in nourishing and protecting our walk with God. We hear little of diligence in a pleasure-oriented society because lust commands more attention than love. Yet, the pathway to God was never meant to veer into rabbit trails of whim and compromise or fall into disrepair by neglect and irresponsibility. Be diligent! **Look for marker #10 which is all about diligently following the Holy Spirit and closely guarding what He says.** He will guide us to the One Who above all is ever diligent.

Inspiration

The society which scorns excellence in plumbing because plumbing is a humble activity and tolerates shoddiness in philosophy because it is an exalted activity will have neither good plumbing nor good philosophy. Neither its pipes nor its theories will hold water.—John Gardner

If God is diligent, surely we ought to be diligent in doing our duty to Him. Think how patient and how diligent God has been with us!—Oswald Chambers in *Not Knowing Where*

Consideration

Marker #10: Diligence
Personal Inventory
I know I am growing in my relationship with
God because I am diligent about:_____

_____

_____

_____

_____

_____

_____

DISCIPLINED

Our Focus

Matthew 26:41—Watch and pray so that you will not fall into temptation. The spirit is willing but the body is weak.

Titus 2:11,12—For the grace of God that brings salvation has appeared to all men. It teaches us to say 'No' to ungodliness and worldly passions, and to live self-controlled, upright and godly lives in this present age, while we wait for the blessed hope—the glorious appearing of our great God and Savior, Jesus Christ.

We could feel the tension increase as the Willamette Star Cruise continued to struggle. What should have taken a few minutes stretched to almost half an hour. The Captain was unable to bring our boat to the dock. Jokes passed across the deck below as some from the wedding party waited to disembark. "Now you can see why I never joined the Navy." "Hmmm, wonder what he's been drinking." "Must be a rookie driver."

What us landlubbers failed to realize was our skipper was fighting a wind. As he tried to ease the boat against the dock, the wind relentlessly pushed us out. It took immense sweat and concentration for him to finally berth the wind-pushed vessel.

How often do we try and improve our relationship with God only to find that we are drifting? So often I come to the end of a day and groan—"O Lord, I did it again. I let the mundane and unnecessary keep me from getting quality time with You."

If I'm in prayer, the struggle is to keep my mind from wandering. The challenge is in listening, and guiding my thoughts so that they are edifying and useful for deepening my relationship with my Father. Spiritual concentration requires effort. If it was as easy as breathing, Jesus would never have had to ask His devoted disciples to watch lest they fall into temptation. He knew within hours of His request they would abandon Him.

During winter Ranger school, a technique my father taught me came in handy for protecting my feet. Dad is a Marine, (you discover in life there's no such thing as "was" a Marine), who fought in the Korean War. Dad's technique for avoiding frostbite during the brutal Korean winter, was to keep a pair of wool socks against his stomach. Whenever his feet were numb or wet with perspiration, he would change into a fresh dry pair. That faithful habit saved his hammer toes from getting nailed by frostbite. Many men wouldn't take the time to carry an extra pair of socks and keep them dry. Their lack of discipline cost them dearly.

Discipline is fundamental to our survival. If we didn't make the effort to drink, eat and sleep right, our bodies would shut down. Discipline is vital for growth. If we want our minds to expand we must make the effort to study. If we want our bodies to be healthy, we must work out!

Spiritual gain requires discipline. God knows how prone we are to forsake "the harder right for the easier wrong"--to disobey laws He established for our welfare. We can work hard doing the wrong things to "be spiritual" and fail miserably. But like the disciplined Captain patiently working against the wind, if we will keep our eyes on Jesus we will grow!

Jesus modeled how to turn away from ungodliness and worldly passions. After a 40 day fast in the desert, He blew apart Satan's temptations with the thundering power of God's Word (Mat.4:4). Every trap the religious establishment set to take Him down failed—they could find no fault in the Son of Man. Jesus met temptation but refused to give in. From the days of Adam to our day, no man or woman has ever been able to mount the platform and capture the gold medal of Perfection except the Lamb of God. He scored only 10's!

Satan cheered His crucifixion and thought His discipline a pathetic waste of time. Heaven roared when He rose up from the grave. He took "just say no" to the limits, loaded the sins of the world on His back and by one perfect sacrifice rocked the gates of hell--permanently. By His example we learn how to live self-controlled, upright and godly lives.

Jesus profoundly changed the life of one of His greatest enemies—Saul. This former religious zealot turned the discipline he had learned from childhood into an all-consuming quest to know and serve Christ. As the Apostle Paul he wrote:

Do you not know that in a race all the runners run, but only one gets the prize? Run in such a way as to get the prize. Everyone who competes in the games goes into strict training. They do it to get a crown that will not last; but we do it to get a crown that will last forever. Therefore I do not run like a man running aimlessly; I do not fight like a man beating the air. No, I beat my body and make it my slave so that after I have preached to others, I myself will not be disqualified for the prize. (1 Co.9:24-27).

Paul taught that the key to spiritual discipline is to make Jesus' core values our core values, His behavior our standard, His instruction our tenets. He is perfect that we can be made perfect.

Saying no to temptation is not easy! Don't expect to run a spiritual race and not get side cramps. The Bible says we can expect to suffer when we seek to be like Jesus. So we need to be prepared! It's little habits like taking the time to carry extra socks that make a big difference over time. Here are spiritual disciplines I work hard to perpetuate to prevent becoming a casualty to sin:

1. **Daily nourishment in God's Word.** The Bible gives me my marching orders, reveals dangers, provides instruction in how to grow, and lets me know how God expects me

to live. Trying to walk the Christian walk without the Bible would be like hang gliding blindfolded.
2. **Consistent time in prayer**—listening to the Holy Spirit, sharing from the heart, confessing where I've blown it.
3. **Weekly fellowship** with other disciplined followers focused on worshiping God.
4. **Weekly accountability** to a ranger buddy—we keep close tabs on our weak areas.

Unfortunately, discipline is not a popular word today. It's much easier to give in to the flesh so we repeatedly break God's commandments because:
➢ someone abused us growing up;
➢ the majority can't be wrong;
➢ living holy costs us popularity;
➢ we need power, position or prominence;
➢ we were born different from others;
➢ God understands and will forgive me;
➢ it's not cool to live a "holier-than-thou" life
➢ it's easier to disobey.

Don't lose heart in your desire to live above the swamp of sin. **"In your struggle against sin, you have not yet resisted to the point of shedding your blood"** (Heb.12:4). **Spiritual discipline is our 11th marker.** It goes beyond diligence in identifying what we ought to do. It is having the courage to walk step-by-step in accordance with God's will through the fog and hardship! Give the Lord your wheel and let Him guide your passage through waves of unending activity and winds of opposition. Set your mind on Him so that you might live in a manner that brings Him glory. It won't come by happenstance. It will take effort and devoted focus.

Inspiration

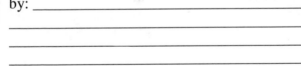

God will not discipline us, we must discipline ourselves. God will not bring every thought and imagination into captivity; we have to do it. Do not say--O Lord, I suffer from wandering thoughts. *Don't* suffer from wandering thoughts.—Oswald Chambers in *My Utmost For His Highest*

Cheap grace is the grace we bestow on ourselves. Cheap grace is the preaching of forgiveness without requiring repentance, baptism without church discipline, communion without confession. Cheap grace is grace without discipleship, grace without the cross, grace without Jesus Christ, living and incarnate. Costly grace ... is the kingly rule of Christ, for whose sake a man will pluck out the eye which causes him to stumble, it is the call of Jesus Christ at which the disciple leaves his nets and follows him.—Dietrich Bonhoeffer in *The Cost of Discipleship*

Consideration

Marker #11: Spiritual Discipline
Personal Inventory

It used to be that I was weak and flaky in my desire to obey God and to seek His presence. But lately, I am working to be more disciplined by: _____

_____

_____

_____

EDIFYING

Our Focus

Colossians 4:7,8--Tychicus will tell you all the news about me. He is a dear brother, a faithful minister and fellow servant in the Lord. I am sending him to you for the express purpose that you may know about our circumstances and that he may encourage your hearts.

Ever thought about starting a Tychicus team? Here are the qualifications a member must possess:

#1. Well-loved by others (it's counterproductive to pick a social recluse).

#2. Faithful minister. This individual has a track record of helping people grow in getting to know God.

#3. Fellow servant in the Lord. An active ingredient in this person is the ability to serve but not from the context of personal agenda—this person serves for the Lord.

#4. Able to travel.

#5. Strong communicator!

#6. Gifted in discernment—this person can identify the condition of the believers with whom he or she fellowships.

#7. An encourager. The result of spending time with this person is edification!

As you can tell, I am a big fan of Tychicus! I wish every spiritual body had at least ten people like him. Whenever Paul needed to encourage young Christians in churches he and others started, he sent good ol' Tych!

A valid way of determining if we are spiritually maturing is gleaned by measuring the effect we have on those around us. If we are growing in godliness, the effect on others should be electric! In truth the more we love God, the greater our capacity should be to encourage those around us, to love them. **This is our 12th marker—the ability to edify**

our brothers and sisters in Christ.

If Tychicus were alive today, he would be buddies with Ron Holechek. Ron is the Director of the Navigator's Military ministry. He is one of those rare individuals who always makes time to listen when a person has the need to share. He asks great questions. He truly cares. Ron is a trainer.

In 1987 Kathleen and I moved to San Diego to go through The Navigator's new staff training Ron led. When we arrived there were only six months left to complete the two year program in which three couples were already enrolled. Ron didn't say, "Forget it, you've missed too much training for us to help you.!" Nor did he ignore us while he completed the other's training. Instead he and his wife Patti poured their lives into helping us just as if we'd been part of the entire process. The Browns, Matthews and Sloans adopted us and made us feel a viable part of the team. That kind of encouraging approach is infectious and motivating! Like Tychicus, Ron is able to serve as a godly influencer over a wide geographical expanse. We all need encouragers around us. And if the Lord is moving in our lives, we will see Him use us to lift the hearts of others!   Amen!

Inspiration

One of the highest of human duties is the duty of encouragement. It is easy to pour cold water on their enthusiasm; it is easy to discourage others. The world is full of discouragers. We have a Christian duty to encourage one another. Many a time a word of praise or thanks or appreciation or cheer has kept a man on his feet.—William Barclay in *The Letter to the Hebrews*

The elderly pastor's wife was known for her ability to make positive comments about every facet of her husband's Florida ministry. The church choir, however, consisting as it did of seniors in their 70s and 80s, had defied positive but truthful comment. She finally solved the problem one Sunday morning. As the choir members filed into the choir loft, she leaned over to me and remarked, "Aren't they walking well this morning?"—Anne Phillips, Ashland, Ohio. "Lite Fare," *Christian Reader*

Blowing out another's candle will not make yours shine brighter.—Cited in *BITS & PIECES*

Consideration
Marker #12: Edifying
Personal Inventory
When I am around other Christians I encourage them by:

_____

_____

_____

_____

_____

FILLED WITH FAITH

Okinawa was a great island on which to begin. My parents took their first steps of missionary faith, moving from the United States to minister to American soldiers stationed there. I remember as a three and four-year old, hiding under the candle-lit table as typhoons roared outside. I recall the fear of deep grass because of the dreaded "step-and-a-half" vipers. (That's how far one could move before falling dead). I caught my first fish on a deep-sea fishing trip. I spent nights agonizing through leg pains brought on by growing. I remember the time we sat around the table and thanked God for the food not understanding that the cupboards were empty. Someone knocked on the door which when opened, yielded a basket of fruit, another time a sack of rice. Life was great after all I was a just a kid. What did I know about struggling? I learned to trust God because that's what my parents did.

Our Focus

John 14:1—Do not let your hearts be troubled. Trust in God; trust also in me.

2 Corinthians 5:7—We live by faith, not by sight.

The more hair I lose the more I understand why Jesus said, "**I tell you the truth, unless you change and become like little children, you will never enter the kingdom of heaven**" (Mat.18:3). As adults our energized pride measures greatness by reasoning and accomplishments. We walk by sight not by faith. But faith is not connect-the-dots living. God never commends us for what we do apart from Him. Faith is an assured impression, a mental realization that the unseen One we love can lead us where we have never been. I now have the joy of watching Bryan, Sarah and Stephen learn about faith.

The cliff broke away like the sloped nose of a roman gladiator. As I walked closer to the edge, his feet stopped moving. Stephen, our youngest, would go no closer. He pulled at my sweater intentionally as if to say, "Forget it, I'm not taking another step!" When I picked him up his arms circled me in pythonic grip. "It's okay," I told him. "I'm not going to let you get hurt." With his gap-toothed grin and an audible sigh he relaxed in my arms. So long as I held him, we could follow the trail beside the clouds and marvel together at the roar of the surf and the whine of the wind.

If we could hear the stories eyes tell, the questions they ask, how wise we would become. For every day, eyes follow our movement, evaluate our behavior and reflect thoughts only God knows. What seems inconsequential in its ordinary state becomes, over time, a powerful treatise to whether faith is any good. How do you act in lines, when deadlines pile up, around a rude co-worker, a screaming child, when your head aches, when the bully throws you down and breaks apart your treasure? Do you bite your lips and grow ill? Do you hang your head like some victory-deficient person? Are you as stable as nitroglycerine? Do you smile and reflect a peace that is surreal? Is your confidence unshakable?

When we reach the maturity to say, "*Lord, my life is in Your hands to do with as You will*", an amazing transformation occurs. We no longer look at the cliff and fear falling. We rest in the security that He Who made us, knows what He is doing.

If we live believing God loves us, our faith goes beyond personal blessing. It is as good as seed in another person's heart. Faith is. Therefore circumstances are secondary. Trials and triumphs are not what matter. Our goal is not to win over the opinions of people. At stake is not being right. We don't have to pretend. There is no reason to quit, no need to doubt. What matters is that we have a simple child-modeled trust in our Father. A trust that blesses all who behold it.

Remember I shared about Bryan's life-threatening tumor? Well, he went through 72 radiation treatments and his tumor shrunk. But I don't believe the radiation saved his life. Virtually every child that received the same treatment he received died within nine months.

Several couples from the Sunday School class I taught in San Diego met in the home of Richard and Joanne Kaiser. We sat with Bryan in a large circle around the living room and prayed for him. We praised God in worship songs and wept. And the Holy Spirit came over us like I have never experienced before or since. During that precious time of worship, I believe God touched my son and spared his life. Today Bryan is both a faithful witness and inspiration to all who have the privilege of knowing him.

Faith is. And in that "is" every eye upon us is brought closer to the One Who is truly awesome. Our faith enables others to become sure that the unseen hands we trust are genuine. So live like you believe, if you say you believe. **Faith is being sure of what we hope for and certain of what we do not see** (Heb.11:1).

Faith is our 13th marker. God, the Cosmic Artist, draws in invisible ink. As we trust Him, life's letters take shape leading us around the next corner. It's like living in Colorado Springs where one never knows what the weather will do next. It is a journey in trust that begins with the first step of confessing I am not in charge—God is! Where He leads, I may not understand but I will follow. I may question what He asks me to do. I may doubt His intentions. I may suggest He let me drive for awhile. But in the end, if I intend to successfully follow Jesus, I must have faith. Something to think about . . . in reveration!

Inspiration

The foundation of spiritual life, for me, has been a high image of God and a high esteem of God—both of which I arrive at by faith.— Frank Laubach in **Practicing His Presence**

Faith never knows where it is being led, it knows and loves the one who is leading. Oswald Chambers in **Not Knowing Where**

Experience is never the ground of my faith; experience is the evidence of my faith. Oswald Chambers in **Conformed to His Image**

Consideration

Marker #13: Faith
Personal Inventory
I know I am growing in my relationship with God because I am exercising faith by:_____

_____

_____

_____

_____

_____

FAITHFUL

Johann* works for Bernard Haldane Associates. As I sat down in his office he said to me, "During the five years I have worked with this company I have interviewed thirty-four pastors. Thirty-three of them missed appointments, were late, or lied when giving information. Only one was a man of integrity." He looked me over as if to say, are you any different. If he meant to get my attention, he succeeded. For the rest of the day I pondered his opening statement and grieved.

I did not get the impression that Johann disdained clergy, or that he was an enemy out to cut down men of the cloth. A former pastor, his love for God is still firmly in place. For that reason alone, his remarks hung in my brain like a withering rain. If Johann was telling the truth and 33 of 34 were obviously found lacking in matters of integrity, what does that say about the condition of our church leaders?

If we are not fervent in our quest to know God, we are set up for moral failure—we are in danger of becoming slackers. To be faithful insists that we "toe the line" of righteousness. To be faithful requires we fulfill our duty before our ever-vigilant King.

*Not his real name

Our Focus

2 Samuel 22:26,27--To the faithful You show Yourself faithful, to the blameless You show Yourself blameless, to the pure You show Yourself pure, but to the crooked You show Yourself shrewd.

Proverbs 20:6--Many a man claims to have unfailing love, but a faithful man who can find?

1 Corinthians 4:2--Now it is required that those who have been given a trust must prove faithful.

I Keep Asking

When I think of faithful I think of the judge who protects the unborn baby despite the pressure of a society that screams "Choice!" I think of the mother who gets up at 3:00 a.m. to attend to her crying baby because she loves her child and recognizes something is wrong. I think of the accountant who ensures that every penny is properly answered for and who would never think of slipping money into her own pocket illegally. I think of the teenager who wakes everyday at the crack of dawn to read her Bible and spend time with her Lord. I think of the senior citizen praying daily for his family that they might walk in holiness before God.

The 14th marker sings out faithful! God's hand on a person's life reveals steadiness, a consistent pattern of doing the right thing from a motivation of love. We all enjoy being around faithful people because they provide security. I would rather have one faithful friend than seventy-five people who are only as trustworthy as a shifting wind.

Jesus needs faithful followers because the world needs Jesus! If you wonder how you are doing in your spiritual journey tackle this question, "Am I faithful?" How would those who know you best answer the question?

Inspiration

We are not responsible for the past generation, and we cannot bear full responsibility for the next one; but we do have our generation. God will hold us responsible as to how well we fulfill our responsibilities to this age and take advantage of our opportunities.—Billy Graham

We have nothing to do with how much ability we've got, or how little, but with what we do with what we have. The man with great talent is apt to be puffed up, and the man with little [talent] to belittle the little. Poor fools! God gives it, much or little. "Our part is to be faithful," doing the level best with every bit and scrap. And we will be if Jesus' spirit controls.—S.D. Gordon in "The Bent-Knee Time", *Christianity Today*, Vol. 32, no. 6.

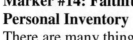

Consideration

Marker #14: Faithful

Personal Inventory

There are many things I do that I do not necessarily enjoy doing, yet, I know God wants me to do them. I work at being faithful by:

_____

_____

_____

_____

FASTING

Our Focus

Isaiah 58:3-9—"Why have we fasted," they say, "and You have not seen it? Why have we humbled ourselves and You have not noticed?" Yet on the day of your fasting, you do as you please and exploit all your workers. Your fasting ends in quarreling and strife, and in striking each other with wicked fists. You cannot fast as you do today and expect your voice to be heard on high. Is this the kind of fast I have chosen, only a day for a man to humble himself? Is it only for bowing one's head like a reed and for lying on sackcloth and ashes? Is that what you call a fast, a day acceptable to the Lord?

Is not this the kind of fasting I have chosen: to loose the chains of injustice and untie the cords of the yoke, to set the oppressed free and break every yoke? Is it not to share your food with the hungry and to provide the poor wanderer with shelter—when you see the naked, to clothe him, and not to turn away from your own flesh and blood? Then your light will break forth like the dawn, and your healing will quickly appear; then your righteousness will go before you, and the glory of the Lord will be your rear guard. Then you will call, and the Lord will answer; you will cry for help, and He will say: Here am I.

Some of the most heated arguments that ever occur happen while people are driving to church! Why is that? And why is it that a person can abstain from food for a whole day in order to get right with God, only to be obnoxious afterwards? Certainly our enemy the devil, loves to do anything he can to disrupt us and keep us from worshiping God with a clean heart. But God, through His prophet Isaiah, in the passage above, reveals deeper insight into our human nature.

Many of the things we do religiously, we do to gain God's attention and approval (often for man's approval as well). We come to God and say, "Look, God, what I did for You. Now how come you haven't noticed?" Please note, worship is not defined by how long we denied ourselves the pleasure of eating on His behalf; by how many hours we spent in prayer; or by how large the check was we slipped in the offering plate. The Pharisees, a powerful religious group in Jesus' day, were the best at fasting, praying and giving. Jesus was not impressed. Why? Because they were legalists more concerned about the law than about how they treated their fellow man. Fasting did not produce in them a greater love for God combined with a desire to put that love in motion. It just inflated their sense of self-importance. They looked great on the outside but were riddled with hypocrisy on the inside.

When I fast it is to let the Lord know how much I love Him. Is there a meal each week, perhaps a day each week you would be willing to set aside in order to fast? Don't make a production out of it, or let it turn into a legal matter. Just simply set aside time to abstain from food to concentrate on your walk with God.

Fasting is marker #15. The key to effective fasting is self-denial not so God will notice me, but that I would notice Him. When my eyes are on Christ, my ears are tuned to the Holy Spirit's frequency and my hands are ready for the Master's work. The grumbling in my stomach isn't complaining; it's the roaring of the engines to get it on— there's holy work to be done!

Inspiration

Biblical fasting always centers on spiritual purposes.—Richard Foster in *Celebration of Discipline*

We must never fast for the sake of direct results . . . The moment we begin to say, 'Because I do this, I get that', it means that we are controlling the blessing. That is to insult God and to violate the great doctrine of His final and ultimate sovereignty. No, we must never advocate fasting as a means of blessing.—D. Martyn Lloyd-Jones in *Studies in the Sermon on the Mount*

Consideration

Marker #15: Fasting
Personal Inventory
I've elected to fast on _____,
so that I might _____
_____
_____
_____
_____

FOCUSED ON CHRIST

You walk outside to pick up your mail when a brilliant flash momentarily blinds you. Before you hovers a Being of glorious light—it is the Lord. You reach out your hand and welcome Him and ask Him to come inside. How exciting you think! This is a chance to show your Savior your home. So you walk Him around. "See, Lord, the beautiful wallpaper we used in our family room. Oh, you must come up and see the hot tub—our favorite hangout. In here is where the kids sleep. Watch out for all the toys—I really wish they'd pick up after themselves. By the way, check out the new wheels in the garage. Isn't this a sweet SUV!"

Time out.

If God descended in bodily form, the first thing you and would do is go from the vertical to the horizontal with the greatest sense of awe and unworthiness that one could muster. When the Lord in His kindness reached down to pick us up, the last thing we would think about is our possessions! Would we think of work or the great meal we just cooked? Come on! All that would matter is the fact that He is present. Our every breath would hang on His next word and action. The whole experience would leave us exhausted—just look at the behavior of Daniel and John (Daniel 10, Revelation 1:17).

Our Focus

Ephesians 5:8-10, 15-17—For you were once darkness, but now you are light in the Lord. Live as children of light (for the fruit of the light consists in all goodness, righteousness and truth) and find out what pleases the Lord . . . Be very careful, then, how you live—not as unwise but as wise, making the most of every opportunity, because the days are evil. Therefore do not be foolish, but understand what the Lord's will is.

Revelation that does not bring us closer to God and make us more aware of our need for Him is most probably not from God and ought to be carefully scrutinized. Spiritual light does more than just part the darkness--it leads us to the King of Brilliance. So if we are mesmerized by mystical experience and constantly on the hunt for new manifestations, we've missed the point. We've given more value to what we feel than to God Himself. If we're enchanted by dynamic dreams but no more deep in our walk with God, then their value and meaning is as rich as vapor.

The absence of revelation is also no hilltop for prancing. Does the Holy Spirit speak to you from the Word, through God-fearers, by His gentle voice? If not, aside from divine purpose, is something blocking Him—like disobedience or fear? Revelation has not ceased! The problem is never in His revealing. The problem is with our hearing. So much noise gets in the way. Are you hungry for a word from the Lord? Great—that's the first essential step.

But what about those times when God seems silent? Three times in my life I have experienced occasions where I had no clue what God's specific purpose for my life entailed. The first time I shared about earlier when I graduated from seminary firmly believing that God was calling me into missions. He did not. He blocked the door and called me into launching a church in another state and pastoring it—something for which I had no experience. I spent a restless year before the Lord made His purpose clear that I was to pastor.

The second and third periods of waiting on God to reveal His will each took almost a year. The danger during each of these times was to conclude that God did not care about me. He did. But often His will takes us in directions we would not have chosen or understood. Often He must work on our character or teach us vital lessons we will need for the next phase of our journey.

The second danger is to think that what makes us important is what we do. It is not. Our value to God is in who we are. What matters most is not that we draw esteem from our work but that we grow in our relationship to Him. It is this very truth that sustains and encourages me during a time of running a race where I have no clue where the road will go next.

The third danger is to grow tired of waiting for God to reveal His purpose and to launch ahead on my own. Solomon wrote in Pro.3:5,6, **"Trust in the Lord with all your heart and lean not on your own understanding; in all your ways acknowledge Him and He will make your paths straight."** Wisdom's child is Patience. Wisdom counsels "wait on God and move as He leads." Why? Because the days are evil and my own understanding is flawed.

If you ever go through a period where more question marks fill the jar than answers, be encouraged. We learn what God's will is by listening and by faithfully spending time with Him. Never despair of finding His purpose. Don't run after euphoria to fill blank spots! Remember Mat.7:7? That's a promise of Christ not a marvelous maybe. If all the world's oceans overflow, it's still true that God has a purpose for you and me! He will reveal it when He's ready. **Marker #16 is our ability to keep looking to Jesus**, not experiences or answers, JESUS!

Inspiration

I am finding every day that the best of the five or six ways in which I try to keep contact with God is for me to wait for His thoughts, to ask Him to speak.—Frank Laubach in *Practicing His Presence*

Our life is full of brokenness—broken relationships, broken promises, broken expectations. How can we live with that brokenness without becoming bitter and resentful except by returning again and again to God's faithful presence in our lives.—Henri Nouwen

A sure sign of spiritual growth is that you take every problem and crisis immediately to Jesus.—David Wilkerson in *"Don't Judge Your Spiritual Condition by Feelings"* 2/19/2001 Newsletter

Consideration
Marker #16: Focused on Christ
Personal Inventory

I know I am growing in my relationship with God because my eyes are on Christ as evidenced by:_____

_____

_____

_____

_____

FORGIVING

> Write injuries in sand, kindness in marble.
> —French Proverb

Do you know people who walk around with a mental rap sheet with the goods on all who have offended, hurt or angered them? I know a man who for years was harassed at a shipping yard by another man who simply did not like him. This person maximized any chance he had to inflict evil on my friend. It made for a tough work environment. Finally, when my friend had taken more abuse than he could stand he went to his management and said either take action against this harasser or I will file a class action suit for having my work place rights violated.

Two days later the supervisor informed him that this man's "head was on his platter". They would terminate his employment if my friend asked. Retribution was his for the taking. But he thought of David when he had opportunity to kill his pursuer King Saul when the king rested in the cave, (see pages 50,51). With the Spirit at work in his heart, he chose not to destroy his enemy but to leave him in God's hands. It was a classy act of forgiveness and one that left a deep impression on the other dock loaders.

Our Focus

Ephesians 4:32--Be kind and compassionate to one another, forgiving each other, just as in Christ God forgave you.

Colossians 3:13--Bear with each other and forgive whatever grievances you may have against one another. Forgive as the Lord forgave you.

Somewhere along the path of walking with God a gorgeous concept takes hold of our hearts and changes forever the way in which we view people. We call it forgiveness. The Apostle Paul wrote the Christians living in Turkey asking them to forgive each other—not because he told them to; not because it was an early church fad; not so they could get their own way; not so people would be impressed! The basis of his asking was the example God set through sending His Forgiver—Jesus! They were to forgive because God forgave them. We are to forgive because God forgave us.

Did we earn His forgiveness—hardly! Does He owe us—absurd! Did He forgive to manipulate us so He could accomplish His agenda—unnecessary! God forgave us on the basis of love! We know this because Eph.4:32 is followed by 5:1,2--**Be imitators of God, therefore, as dearly loved children and live a life of love, just as Christ loved us and gave Himself up for us as a fragrant offering and sacrifice to God.**

Friends, one of the greatest feelings you can experience is to truly forgive someone else. The exercise of forgiveness is the expression of love! Are you carrying resentment against another person? Jesus said, **"And when you stand praying, if you hold anything against anyone, forgive him, so that your Father in heaven may forgive you your sins"** (Mark 11:25). Are you fed up with those who repeatedly wrong you? Peter seemed to think there ought to be a limit as to how much a person should forgive another. He asked, **"Lord, how many times shall I forgive my brother when he sins against me? Up to seven times?"** Jesus rocked his boat by replying, **"I tell you, not seven times, but seventy-seven times"** (Mat.18:21,22).

Marker #17 is a great indicator that we are becoming more God-like for we understand how undeserving we are of God's forgiveness. Therefore, **in humility, consider it a joy to forgive those who have hurt us**.

Inspiration

Forgiveness is the fragrance that the flower leaves on the heel of the one who crushed it.—Mark Twain

Forgiveness is made possible by the knowledge that human beings cannot offer us what only God can give.—Henri J. M. Nouwen in "Forgiveness: The Name Of Love In a Wounded World", *Weavings* March/April 1992

Bear and forbear.—Epictetus

It is manlike to punish but godlike to forgive.—Peter Von Winter

Consideration

Marker #17: Forgiving
Personal Inventory
I know I am growing in my relationship with God because I am able to forgive:

_____

_____

_____

_____

_____

GENEROUS

There are few things which reveal a person's heart so well as money. Consider the rich young man Jesus met (Mat.19:16-22). He honestly wondered what good thing he must do to gain life without end. He faithfully kept God's commandments. Jesus said, **"If you want to be perfect, go, sell your possessions and give to the poor, and you will have treasure in heaven. Then come, follow Me."** Faced with the prospect of relinquishing his wealth, the rich man sadly departed.

If variety is the spice of life, money is the main course. A rich man could not let go of his possessions to gain eternal life. How tragically absurd! Why would a sincere man forfeit his ability to gain eternal life to enjoy a fleeting affair with finances?

There is nothing corrupt about coins or currency. Money is a necessary commodity for acquiring goods or services. What is dangerous is the excessive preoccupation people have for it. Money can affect the poor as much as the rich for craving can be as debilitating as clutching. Is it this unhealthy fixation which birthed the saying, "Money is the root of all evil?" As defined in the **American Heritage Dictionary**, consider three of the most visible tentacles which protrude from this over-watered root:

Greed—"An excessive desire to acquire or possess more than what one needs or deserves, especially with respect to material wealth."

Stinginess—"implies absence of generosity and often an inclination toward meanness of spirit."

Idolatry—"Blind or excessive devotion to something."

If you believe you have a healthy handle on money you are a blessed person. No doubt you are experiencing the fruit of joy that comes from being generous. But before you or I merrily proceed down the path of bliss, we ought to consider this: A close examination of Scripture reveals that the

Israelites were expected to give well beyond 10% of their income to God and His work.

Our Focus

Proverbs 11:25,28—A generous man will prosper; he who refreshes others will himself be refreshed . . . Whoever trusts in his riches will fall, but the righteous will thrive like a green leaf.

Psalm 37:25,26—I was young and now I am old, yet I have never seen the righteous forsaken or their children begging bread. They are always generous and lend freely; their children will be blessed.

It was a sad day for Jesus when the rich man walked away. It will be a sad day again if we forsake the cost of discipleship for the accumulation of wealth. There is a world out there starving to hear the good news, desperate for Bibles in their own languages, hungry for someone to come and teach words of life. They're not interested in how comfortable we are. Neither is Jesus, Who said, "**If any man would come after Me he must deny himself and take up his cross daily and follow Me**" (Luke 9:23). The word was deny not delight.

Some time ago, I read a letter from missionaries to a Micronesian island who receive the **Reveration** devotional. They wrote,

> If only our Christian family back home could spend time with us on the battle front to see the hunger and thirst and the darkness on these tropical rainforest islands. If so, then they would forgo their second cars, pools, exotic holidays, retirement savings. We even had one person say to us they would love to support us (they are extremely well off), but they needed to make sure they had all their retirement in order first. Another person said

they didn't want to be around us because they were afraid that the Lord may call them to sell everything and go to a mission field.

Ouch!

Perhaps no one has ever challenged you. So here's a self-test I encourage you to take.

♦ Am I willing to give at least 10% of my income to further the Lord's work?

♦ What thoughts go through my mind when asked to give?

♦ Do the gears of rationalization begin turning?

♦ Do I resent that this subject has been raised and wish to avoid it altogether?

♦ Am I too attached to my lifestyle and income to make sacrifices?

♦ Do I give only when it is convenient?

♦ Do I know how to give sacrificially?

How you and I answer these questions will reveal much about our character and how we are influenced by money. Don't fall victim to present temptations at the expense of future blessings. **Marker #18 reveals our ability to live generously.** Our hearts are aligned with God's will so that His work is furthered. Jesus promised:

Everyone who has left houses or brothers or sisters or father or mother or children or fields for My sake will receive a hundred times as much and will inherit eternal life" (Mat.19:29).

Now that's what I call a dividend!

Inspiration

The more you have the less you can give, and the less you have the more you can give.—Mother Teresa

When we discuss money, we're talking about commitment, and commitment is our domain.—Haddon Robinson

The wise man does not lay up treasure. The more he gives the more he has.—Chinese proverb

Jesus talked much about money. Sixteen of the thirty-eight parables were concerned with how to handle money and possessions. In the Gospels, an amazing one out of ten verses (288 in all) deal (sic) directly with the subject of money. The Bible offers 500 verses on prayer, less than 500 verses on faith, but more than 2,000 verses on money and possessions.—Howard L. Dayton, Jr.

Consideration

Marker #18: Generous
Personal Inventory
I know I am growing in my relationship with God because I am giving to:_____

_____

_____

_____

_____

_____

HABITUAL

Dear Abby: I am forty-four and would like to meet a man my age with no bad habits.—Rose

Dear Rose: So would I.

The sun was blinding as it reflected off the snow on the high plateau on which Denver sits. As I got into the car I wondered what it would be like driving without sunglasses. Automatically, I reached up to grab the clutch that switches the car from park into drive. Instead the windshield was coated with cleansing fluid and the wipers did their dance across the glass. Oh! The rental car was definitely not like my Ford Taurus. The clutch for the automatic transmission sat below and to my right. For the next two days I laughed as I continuously turned on the wipers—oh, the power of habit!

Our Focus

Matthew 7:24—Therefore everyone who hears these words of mine and puts them into practice is like a wise man who built his house on the rock.

When Jesus Christ becomes our Lord, we expectantly look for Him to change our lives and He does but not without our help. That foul language that punctuates our speech, the cigarette we naturally grab for, the temper that flashes to the surface with volcanic regularity . . . these habits rarely vanish when we climb into the vehicle with our Savior to drive where He wants us to go. We must make the conscious effort to say no to whatever is not right, to embrace that which pleases God. It takes time, effort, patience and faith to build godly habits. God wants us to be holy. We must be willing to make those decisions and take the heroic actions that result in obedience to the will of our Lord. **This is our 19th marker—becoming habitual in godly things.**

As I review my relationship with God I have found certain habits are indispensable. See if this list sounds familiar!

1. Daily time invested in God's Word. If I don't read/ study/meditate in the Bible each day, I miss a spiritual meal—holy nutrition. What is amazing is I may eat from the word today and not feel nourished. But a month from now, the Holy Spirit may bring to mind those verses exactly when I need them!

2. Daily time invested in prayer. If I don't pray I can count on the fact that my stress level will go higher, my day will be more frustrating and I will feel disconnected from God. Conversely, if I pray, the trials that arise seem less annoying, I'm able to encourage others by my own uplifted spirit and I feel more in touch with the Lord.

3. Worship. There is something incredibly uplifting about gathering regularly with other Christians to fellowship and celebrate God. Without worship, the very air I breathe seems stale. I make it a practice to let the Lord know how much I love Him!

I'm sure there are numerous other things that could be added to the list. The point is that without establishing these essentials, my spiritual life has as much flavor as tofu. By the grace of God, fight to establish what will deepen your love for God. By His mercy, resist anything that keeps you from pleasing your Savior!

Inspiration

It seems, in fact, as though the second half of a man's life is made up of nothing but the habits he has accumulated during the first half.—Fyodor Dostoevsky

We first make our habits, and then our habits make us.—John Dryden

I Keep Asking

Sow an act and you reap a habit. Sow a habit and you reap a character. Sow a character and you reap a destiny.—Charles Reade

Habits are at first cobwebs, then cables.—Spanish Proverb

Consideration
Marker #19: Good Habits
Personal Inventory
These are the habits God is helping me maintain:_____

_____

_____

_____

_____

_____

INSIGHTFUL

> The purpose of a fish trap is to catch fish and when the fish are caught, the trap is forgotten. The purpose of a rabbit snare is to catch rabbits. When the rabbits are caught, the snare is forgotten. The purpose of the word is to convey ideas. When the ideas are grasped, the words are forgotten. Where can I find a man who has forgotten words? He is the one I would like to talk to.—Chuang Tzu

Sometimes in counseling a person a thought will cross my mind that I know is from the Lord. How do I know it is from the Lord? First, it is not something I would normally think up. Second, when I share it with the person it will minister in a profound way. It really thrills me to know that the Lord of all creation is willing to make Himself available to help us grow!

We cannot have enough of God can we! The more we discover of Him, the more we realize how little we know. It is pretty fantastic that there is no cap, no finite limit to what we may learn. Therefore it is our challenge and our privilege to walk this sin-plagued planet seeking the Lord's wisdom.

As I look back in time there are a few key lessons that rise to the surface—many of which still effect me significantly today. These lessons, or insights, help me see that I am maturing. Not long ago, I read nuggets of truth a godfather was sharing with a special young woman to help her through life. The thoughts of this sage inspired me to consider what treasured lessons God has used in my heart to help me grow.

#1. When in doubt don't. My nature is to be impetuous. I guess it goes along with being an idea person. When it comes to interacting with people I'm ready to give advice and sometimes plenty of it. God is teaching me to be quiet.

Sometimes people need to struggle and my tinkering keeps them from learning lessons God has for them.

There are times when I would like to take action at work or in ministry. But I have learned not to make any major decisions without first getting permission from the Lord. That "okay" may come from Scripture, strong leading of the Holy Spirit, advice from mentors and close friends, circumstances, or a combination of the preceding. I will be covering these in more detail in *I Pray Also*. If I have doubt about something, I've learned to stay put. When the time is right to take action, the Lord makes it clear.

#2. My purpose in life is to please God not necessarily people. I used to find that the biggest challenge on Sunday morning was not how well I delivered the message but rather what temperature the thermostat was set on. Invariably one group was too cold while another was too warm. I learned to acknowledge the complaint or suggestion of people but leave the control knob alone. In other words, I did not say whether I agreed or not with them, I just let them know their concern was heard. It is not possible to please everyone and it is not necessary.

My responsibility is not to be popular but to be obedient. Often what the church and Christians need is change. We become complacent and set in our ways. God uses change to keep us looking to Him, to help us be more relevant to those around us who don't know Him. But people naturally resist change. Leaders have to be willing to move folks out of their comfort zone if God is asking for change. Followers have to be willing to forgo personal perks to support godly leaders.

#3. God is not in the cloning business. For the first several years of my marriage, I tried to change Kathleen. While my motives may have been good, my approach to her was harmful. I wanted her to be a people-person like me. I expected her to open our home continuously for ministry because that's what my home was like growing up. I missed the wisdom and gifts she brought to our marriage because I was too busy trying to "be right". Being with people energizes me. Being with people wears her down. Just because she views things differently than I do does not make her wrong or right. In fact the issue often is not who is right but rather who is honoring.

My responsibility is to honor her for her differences, adjust my way of thinking and recognize that God put us together to make us stronger. It is precisely because my wife is not like me that we have an organized, well-cared for home. My children are gaining an awesome education from their mother. I am able to minister in ways I could never have managed because of her gifts.

In the same way, we need to be careful to recognize the diversity of personalities, talents and gifts God has placed in the body. If we would spend less time trying to get people to conform to our expectations and more time looking for the strengths those around us contribute, we would become much more productive and joyful!

#4. The lesson of the fir tree. In Oregon majestic fir trees tower high into the sky. They provide wonderful shade and stay a beautiful dark green all year. They also have a weakness that is not so well known. Perhaps because of the rainy climate in the Northwest, firs do not put down deep roots. For this reason it is never a good idea to grow a single fir, or chop down a grove to leave a couple tress standing. They might just come crashing down in a wind storm. When firs are planted together their roots interlock. Consequently, their strength is in numbers.

I don't believe God wants us to negotiate life alone. Like with fir trees our strength is in community. In Scripture we find repeatedly that teams are the way to go! There is strength in numbers (Ecc. 4:12). When personalities and talents are combined the whole becomes greater than the sum of the parts.

#5. Insecurity is the foundation of gossip. It is a great blotch on our reputations as ambassadors of Christ the way we talk about others. I am increasingly amazed at how quickly Satan can destroy the body of Christ by stoking conversation that is less than edifying. Gossip comes from feeling insecure about who we are. When we point out others shortcomings, it's as if we are raising our own stature. In fact the opposite is true. Gossip reveals how weak we are. The closer I grow to the Lord, the more I find He checks me from speaking. Words have the power to hurt and to heal. If I have not spoken directly to the person whose behavior or character I question, I have no business speaking to others about that person. To do so breaks down trust and love.

#6. A joyful spirit is medicine to a weary world. It is awesome to be in love with God. A life that adores Him is like a waterfall. The sight, sound and feeling is inspiring. I try to live my life each day full of joy. I intentionally aim to bring the presence of the Lord into my surroundings. Consequently, I see Him use me to encourage others. But my eyes must be on Christ to do this. I believe that if I would all work to relate to our Father throughout each day, people would come running to have what we have—true joy!

Marker #20 spots our insightful ability to see people, events and circumstances as God sees them.

So, we have now passed twenty markers. There are plenty more to come. I hope you are enjoying the journey . . . growing in knowing . . . loving the Lord with all your heart! I keep asking. I hope you will too! May you know Him better. Something to think about . . . in reveration!

Our Focus

Philippians 1:9-11—And this is my prayer: that your love may abound more and more in knowledge and depth of insight, so that you may be able to discern what is best and may be pure and blameless until the day of Christ, filled with the fruit of righteousness that comes through Jesus Christ—to the glory and praise of God.

Inspiration

The three foundations of learning: Seeing much, suffering much, and studying much.—Catherall

Spiritual insight is not for the purpose of making us realize we are better than other people, but in order that our responsibility might be added to.—Oswald Chambers in *The Pilgrim's Song Book*

Men are four:

He who knows not and knows not he knows not, he is a fool—shun him;

He who knows not and knows he knows not, he is simple—teach him;

He who knows and knows not he knows, he is asleep—wake him;

He who knows and knows he knows, he is wise—follow him!—Arabic Apothegm

Consideration

Marker #20: Insightful
Personal Inventory

I know I am growing in my relationship with God because He has given me insight into:

_____

_____ _____

_____

_____

CONCLUSION

Our Focus

2 Peter 1:3—His divine power has given us everything we need for life and godliness through our knowledge of Him Who called us by His own glory and goodness.

Did you know that you have a permanent account in the Bank Of Heaven? God promises us that through His power He has given us everything we need to live, everything we need to be godly. This power is made available to us through our knowledge of Him. The closer we grow to God, the better we are able to draw from Him whatever we need to have an abundant life! You and I cannot exhaust God's resources. Now tell me seriously, do we not have an incredible Lord!

I hope this book has encouraged you in your quest to know your Father. I hope you will share it with someone else negotiating the path of life looking to know God better. As mentioned earlier, *I Keep Asking* is the first book of a two-book series on spiritual growth. The second book, *I Pray Also* covers tools God gives us to grow, subtle obstacles to spiritual growth, and twenty more markers that help us determine if we are in fact growing. You can purchase copies of either book by filling out the order form on the last page. Now may God bless you and equip you to be a child in whom His glory is radiated!

Final Inspiration

God does not give us overcoming life; He gives us life as we overcome . . . If we will do the overcoming, we shall find we are inspired of God because He gives life immediately.—Oswald Chambers in *My Utmost For His Highest*

Appendix 1—Definitions

Except for words coined by the author, all definitions are taken from **The American Heritage Dictionary of the English Language.** Third Edition ©1992 by Houghton Mifflin Company.

ab•ne•ga•tion *n.* Self-denial.

con•cu•pis•cence *n.* A strong desire, especially sexual desire; lust. **--con•cu"pis•cent** *adj.*

dif•fi•dent *adj.* **1.** Lacking or marked by a lack of self-confidence; shy and timid.

dis•sem•ble *v.* **dis•sem•bled, dis•sem•bling, dis•sem•bles.** --*tr.* **1.** To disguise or conceal behind a false appearance. See Synonyms at **disguise. 2.** To make a false show of; feign. --*intr.* To disguise or conceal one's real nature, motives, or feelings behind a false appearance.

eu•phe•mism *n.* The act or an example of substituting a mild, indirect, or vague term for one considered harsh, blunt, or offensive: *"Euphemisms such as 'slumber room' . . . abound in the funeral business"* (Jessica Mitford).

Ha•la•kah also **Ha•la•cha** *n.* *Judaism.* The legal part of Talmudic literature, an interpretation of the laws of the Scriptures.

hu•mon•gous or **hu•mun•gous** *adj.* *Slang.* Extremely large; enormous: *"humongous baked potatoes piled high with sour cream"* (Boston Globe).

im•bro•glio *n.* **1.a.** A difficult or intricate situation; an entanglement. **b.** A confused or complicated disagreement. **2.** A confused heap; a tangle.

im•pal•pa•ble *adj.* **1.** Not perceptible to the touch; intangible. **2.** Difficult to perceive or grasp by the mind.

in•do•lence *n.* Habitual laziness; sloth.

plan•chette *n.* A small triangular board supported by two casters and a vertical pencil which, when lightly touched by the fingertips, is said to spell out subconscious or supernatural messages.

Po vil ity *n.* The blessed state of humbly recognizing my inadequacy before my Lord, poor in spirit—a word coined by the author.

pru•ri•ent *adj.* **1.** Inordinately interested in matters of sex; lascivious. **2.a.** Characterized by an inordinate interest in sex: *prurient thoughts.* **b.** Arousing or appealing to an inordinate interest in sex: *prurient literature.*

quin•tes•sence *n.* **1.** The pure, highly concentrated essence of a thing. **2.** The purest or most typical instance: *the quintessence of evil.*

Reveration *n.* Reverent adoration for God—a word coined by the author.

sa•gac•i•ty *n.* The quality of being discerning, sound in judgment, and farsighted; wisdom.

APPENDIX 2—FEEDBACK

Now that you have read *I Keep Asking,*

Please visit our web page at www.encounterministries.com
to:

    ✐let us know what you think of the book
    ✐sign up to receive your free weekly devotional--
        Reveration
    ✐see what others are saying
    ✐e-mail the author

or

    ✐Write to:
    Dan York
    Encounter Ministries
    12350 S.W. Tiedeman Ave.
    Tigard, OR 97223-4025

APPENDIX 3—BIBLE ABBREVIATIONS USED

OLD TESTAMENT

Genesis—Gen.
Leviticus—Lev.
Deuteronomy—Deu.
Joshua—Jos.
1 Samuel—1 Sa.
1 Chronicles—1 Ch.
Psalms—Psa.
Proverbs—Pro.
Ecclesiastes—Ecc.
Isaiah—Isa.
Jeremiah—Jer.

NEW TESTAMENT

Matthew—Mat.
Romans—Rom.
1 Corinthians—1 Co.
2 Corinthians—2 Co.
Galatians—Gal.
Ephesians—Eph.
Philippians—Php.
Colossians—Col.
Hebrews—Heb.
1 Peter—1 Pe.
1 John—1 Jo.

BIBLE VERSIONS USED

NIV—New International Version
NKJV—New King James Version ©1982 Thomas Nelson Inc.
Nashville, TN
NLT—New Living Translation

BOOKs by **Oswald Chambers** can be ordered through Discovery House Publishers 1-800-653-8333.

Book Source Material

Written inspirational quotes (except for those already noted from published magazines) taken from published authors:

Abraham, Marilyn J. *First We Quit Our Jobs.* Dell Trade Paperback, 1997.

Barclay, William. *The Letter to the Hebrews.* Philadelphia: The Westminster Press, 1976.

Barnhouse, Donald Gray. *Revelation.* Zondervan Publishing House, 1985.

Bevere, John. *The Fear of the Lord.* Creation House, 1997.

Blackaby, Henry T. & Claude V. King. *Experiencing God.* Broadman & Holman Publishers, 1994.

Bonhoeffer, Dietrich. *The Cost of Discipleship.* New York: MacMillan, 1960.

J. Budziszewski, *The Revenge of Conscience: Politics and the Fall of Man.* Spence Publishing Company, 2000.

Collins, Gary. *Christian Counseling.* Word Incorporated, 1980.

Chambers, Oswald. *Approved Unto God* (1997); *Biblical Ethics* (1998); *Christian Disciplines* (1995); *Conformed to His Image* (1996); *Disciples Indeed* (1998); *God's Workmanship* (1997); *He Shall Glorify Me* (1997); *If You Will Ask* (1989); *My Utmost For His Highest* (1963); *Not Knowing Where* (1989); *Shadow of an Agony* (1992); *So Send I You* (1951); *Studies in the Sermon on the Mount* (1960); *The Love of God Volume: Now Is It Possible* (1988); *The Moral Foundations of Life* (1998); *The Pilgrim's Song Book* (1992); *The Place of Help* (1989); *The Servant as His Lord* (1996); *The Shadow of an Agony* (1992); Oswald Chambers Publications Association Limited.

Downer, Phil. *A Father's Reward.* Harvest House Publishers, 1998.

BOOK SOURCE MATERIAL CONT.

Foster, Richard. *Celebration of Discipline*. San Francisco: Harper & Row, Publishers, 1978

Guiness, Os. *The Call*. Nashville: Word Publishing, 1998.

Hybels, Bill. *Too Busy Not to Pray*. InterVarsity Press, 1988.

Lawrence, Brother & Frank Laubach. *Practicing His Presence*. The SeedSowers, 1973.

Lloyd-Jones, D. Martyn. *Studies in the Sermon on the Mount*. Grand Rapids: WM.B. Eerdmans Publishing Company, 1977.

Murray, Andrew. *The New Life*. Minneapolis: Bethany Fellowship, Inc., 1965.

Nee, Watchman. *Spiritual Authority*. New York: Christian Fellowship Publishers, Inc., 1972.

Packer, J.I. *Knowing God*. InterVarsity Press, 1993.

Sanders, J. Oswald. *A Spiritual Clinic*. Chicago: Moody Press, 1961.

Schultz, Duane. *The Maverick War: Chennault and the Flying Tigers*. New York: St. Martin's Press, 1987.

Sproul, R.C. *The Glory of Christ*. Wheaton: Tyndale House Publishers, Inc., 1990.

Swindoll, Charles. *three steps forward two steps back*. New York: Bantam Books, 1980.

The Cadet Prayer. Bugle Notes 1977-1981

Thielicke, Helmut. *The Silence of God*. Grand Rapids: William B. Eerdmans Publishing Company, 1966.

Tozer, A.W. *The Divine Conquest*. Tyndale House Publishers Inc., 1995.

Wilkerson, David. *America's Last Call*. Wilkerson Trust Publications, 1998.

Wilkinson, Bruce. *The Prayer of Jabez*. Multnomah Publishers, Inc., 2000.

NOTES

I Keep Asking

NOTES

keep asking that the God of our Lord Jesus Christ, the glorious Father, may give you the Spirit of wisdom and revelation, so that you may know Him better"—**Ephesians 1:17**.

Read what others have to say about Dan's writings:

"Your meditations over the years have been timely . . . Please pray for me and for the work the Potter is doing on the wheel."—Former Missionary to Thailand.

"Just a short note to let you know that a friend of ours has been faithfully sending your Reverations to us for over a year now and we have thoroughly enjoyed them and been encouraged by them. Thank you."—Missionaries on the island of Pohnpei

"Thanks for all the Reveration pieces. I save them all."—Marine veteran with The Navigators

"Thanks for being a blessing to us."—African reader from Ghana

"Most heartfelt thank you! I needed this message going through the valley of tears."—Soldier in the U.S. Army

"I have received your devotions for two years now, and they are a constant encouragement."—Housewife in Texas

"Yet again another fitting message for my life right now."—Nike employee

"Bless your heart! Once again, you've done an outstanding job with the truth."—Pastor in northern California

"Thanks for all the encouraging devotions. They help me tremendously in all aspects of life. The best part is that they are basic concepts brought into new light."—Businessman in Washington

ABOUT THE AUTHOR

Daniel York is the Director of Encounter Ministries and continues to co-pastor Light of Christ Community Church, the second church he has planted in Tigard, Oregon. Dan grew up a missionary kid (mk), living in Okinawa, Korea, Japan and the Philippines as well as throughout the United States.

In 1977, he graduated from Faith Academy in the Philippines, and was congressionally appointed to West Point from which he graduated and was commissioned an officer in the United States Army in 1981. He continues to serve in the Army Reserves.

Besides his love for worship, Dan enjoys parenting, speaking, writing, sports evangelism, and coaching people in ministry. His joy in the Lord is profoundly contagious.

Stephen, Kathleen, Bryan, Sarah and Dan

ORDER FORM

On-line orders: www.encounterministries.com (save additional $2.25 on order)

Telephone orders: Call (503) 620-4081

Postal Orders: **Encounter Ministries**
12350 S.W. Tiedeman Ave.
Tigard, OR 97223-4025

I Keep Asking	**$11.95**	=	$_____
I Pray Also (Available winter of 2001)			
	$12.95	=	$_____
Of Seen and Unseen (Worship Songs CD)			
(Available winter of 2001)	**$15.95**	=	$_____
Choices (Seeker/Discipleship Songs CD)			
	$13.95	=	$_____
Choices Tape	**$7.95**	=	$_____
Salt (Discipleship Songs CD)	**$9.95**	=	$_____

SHIPPING AND HANDLING:

Please include $3.95 for first book/CD and $1.00 for each additional book or CD   **Total:** = $_____

Payment: ☐ Check   Credit Card: ☐Visa
☐MasterCard   ☐Discover   ☐Am. Express

Please Print:

Card number:_____

Exp. date:_____ /_____

Name on Card:_____

Signature:_____

SEND BOOK(s) TO:
Name:_____
Address:_____
City:_____
State_____ ZIP_____
Phone: (_____)_____
Personalize book to:
_____

**Call now and order at
1-503-620-4081**